Contents

Facilitating Organisational Change in Primary Care

A manual for team members

Marion Duffy and **Elaine Griffin**

Tayside Centre for General Practice
University of Dundee

RADCLIFFE MEDICAL PRESS

© 2000 Tayside Centre for General Practice

Radcliffe Medical Press
18 Marcham Road, Abingdon, Oxon OX14 1AA

ISBN 1 85775 495 6

Typeset by Joshua Associates Ltd, Oxford
Printed and bound by TJ International Ltd, Padstow, Cornwall

Preface

In recent years general practice has provided an almost constant experience of change, much of it imposed.

Having been asked to become team based, to embrace new technology, audit and manage clinical care according to multi-disciplinary protocols, practices are now required to produce practice development plans, engage actively in their local health care co-operative or primary care group and institute clinical governance mechanisms.

There are many guides and manuals available, offering techniques for improving teamwork and for instigating and managing change – from *team development kits* to *SWOT analysis* to *needs assessment* to *action planning*. Few of these take a 'step back' to discuss **who** will guide the process and **what skills and knowledge** those people will need. Facilitator posts are advertised and often filled by individuals with clinical backgrounds, who find a plethora of guides to managing change in Japanese car factories but a dearth of written material contextualised for their own setting!

In the first volume of this series, *Facilitating Groups in Primary Care*, our aim was to equip those individuals working in primary care with an understanding of how people work together in groups and how they can be helped to do that more effectively. In this accompanying volume, we build on that foundation and encourage the reader to concentrate on how organisations work and on how they impact on their members, suggesting that facilitation can be a valuable life skill in the organisational development process.

This book draws on the experience of a number of research and development projects managed from the Tayside Centre for General Practice, University of Dundee, and is grounded in the work of modern-day general practice in the United Kingdom. It does contain tips and techniques for managing change – but its central purpose is to equip those individuals working in general practice with an understanding of how facilitation can effect the successful acceptance and management of change. With that aim in mind, it should be of benefit to any member of the primary care team, but in particular to any holding the title 'Facilitator'.

Marion Duffy
Elaine Griffin
April 2000

List of tools

- Force field analysis
- Paradigm shift
- Nominal group technique
- Responsibility charting
- Action planning
- Why worry?
- Domainal map
- Characterise your practice
- Team diagnostic summary
- Communication audit
- Best practice
- SWOT analysis
- Computer tasks and skills analysis
- Away-day planning
- Ice breakers
- Setting objectives for a group activity or meeting
- Brainstorming
- Summarising
- Giving feedback
- A process for reflection

List of case studies

Acknowledgements

The authors gratefully acknowledge the financial support of Roche Pharmaceuticals, without whose sponsorship this handbook, its predecessor, *Facilitating Groups in Primary Care*, and their accompanying workshops would not have been developed at this time. Roche responded to a need identified by the authors for a handbook for those working in primary care which was contextualised for that setting. Facilitation posts are increasingly being advertised by health care organisations. Those who take on the task find little published material to help support their own development in the role. Additionally, practice-based professionals need to develop facilitation skills so that they can maximise the effectiveness of teamworking, so as to manage the changing demands of the organisation and provision of healthcare.

Eight general medical practices from the Tayside and Grampian regions of Scotland participated in the workshops which accompanied the development of this handbook. Their active engagement in the process of skill development and their feedback on the relevance and value of both the handbook and the training have been of considerable benefit to the authors. We extend our thanks to them.

Fifteen general medical practices in Tayside participated in the project entitled 'Facilitating Education and Development' (the FED project). Many of the case studies in this handbook are based on experiences during that project, although some details have been altered to ensure confidentiality. We acknowledge the practices' willing co-operation in that project.

We would also like to thank colleagues at Tayside Centre for General Practice and Tayside Audit Resource for Primary Care (TARPC) for sharing their past experiences of using facilitation as a tool for personal and practice development. In particular we mention Arlene Napier, who gave generously of her time and resources in the development of the content for the manual.

And finally, we must acknowledge the support and encouragement of our own families who showed considerable stoicism during the writing of this second volume. They could well remember the effects on family life during the writing of volume 1! Thank you for your encouragement and practical support.

Chapter 1

Facilitating groups in primary care: qualities, skills and opportunities

Summary

In this chapter we summarise the key messages contained in volume 1 of this series of books about facilitation, Facilitating Groups in Primary Care (Duffy and Griffin, 1999). There we identified opportunities to facilitate one's own group, whether in a formal facilitation role or by acting in a generally more facilitative way, and outlined some of the key personal qualities and interpersonal skills required to meet the demands of the role.

Sections of this chapter highlight:

- the essential qualities of a Facilitator
- opportunities to facilitate within your own group
- maximising the benefit of working in groups
- the need for reflection using a structured reflective framework.

The essential qualities of a Facilitator

In different settings, and in a variety of ways, Facilitators help groups function more effectively. A useful way to describe their work comes from Bentley (1994):

> *Facilitation is the provision of opportunity, resources, encouragement and support for the group to succeed in achieving its own objectives and to do this through enabling the group to take control and responsibility for the way they proceed.*

In the health service, Facilitators have helped groups by offering a wide range of practical assistance and moral support. They have provided ideas, information, advice, direction, resources, support, training and tools. Facilitators have worked with practices in areas of both clinical and organisational development.

Facilitators' skills are rooted in a desire and commitment to work for the benefit of the particular group or organisation and in an understanding of how the effectiveness of group processes can be maximised through attention paid to certain key aspects of:

- planning
- making sense of what is going on
- structuring activities
- dealing with difficult issues
- promoting the well-being of the group
- recognising the achievements of the group.

The predominant skills and qualities are typically described as being:

- flexibility of style
- respect for the autonomy of others
- honesty, reliability
- neutrality and objectivity
- sensitivity to others, empathy
- caring, warmth and genuineness in approach
- knowledge of the context and of group processes
- ability to provide orientation in the course of work
- enthusiasm and positive attitude to the job in hand
- in possession of a repertoire of techniques and tools for interpersonal and group development
- skill in dealing with conflict.

Regardless of title, **anyone** working in a group can demonstrate, and make deliberate use of, such skills and qualities for the benefit of that group.

Opportunities to facilitate within your own group in primary care

When working in groups in primary care you may be given the opportunity to take on the formal role of Facilitator. This will entail acting in a slightly different way from normal and the exact role should be made explicit to others so that there is no confusion. For example, you may facilitate a review of practice meetings to assess and improve upon their effectiveness. You might also formally set up a new group, working with that group to establish its mode of operation. You may take on the task of organising and facilitating a practice 'away-day'. Whatever the situation, your role will be to attend to those practical tasks which create a suitable environment in which to work together – the room layout, the timing, the refreshments, the necessary documents, etc. – *and* to provide structure, orientation, tools, training, support, resources, interventions and motivation, as necessary, to maximise the benefits of working in that group.

When acting in this formal role, you need to be able to work with, and for, the group without either dominating it or being dominated by it, without imposing your own personal agenda or following your own needs.

Where many primary healthcare teams or practice groups have a need for facilitation is in the **process** of working together. Time and other pressures tend to result in a strong focus on the **task** element – meeting deadlines for action, producing documents such as development plans, organising new clinics. Scant attention is paid to issues such as:

- the preferred way of working together
- the goals of the group
- full participation by all group members
- dealing with differences in opinion
- ensuring that agreement is real and not superficial
- reviewing the operation of the group.

The use of **facilitative interventions** will probably be the aspect of the facilitator role least familiar to you. These interventions – deliberate verbal and sometimes non-verbal responses to a group situation – can help the group in the following ways:

- set the climate
- manage time

- ensure active participation
- maintain energy and alertness
- create the future
- draw out issues
- keep to the task
- deal with unhelpful behaviour
- articulate what is not being said
- identify agreement and disagreement
- encourage learning in the group
- give and receive feedback
- complete an activity.

(after Hunter *et al.*, 1996)

Even if not in the formal Facilitator role, you can nevertheless be a more facilitative group member by understanding the nature of working in groups, by behaving in ways which will help the group to function more effectively and by suggesting the use of appropriate tools for the group to use to improve its way of working.

Maximising the benefit of working in groups

Groups have the potential to maximise the benefits of working together if they pay attention to the **process** of working together as well as focusing on the **task** in hand. Certain types of behaviour will help get the job done – proposing strategies for action, seeking others' opinions, summarising discussion, clarifying issues. Other actions help the group work together well – encouraging others, being friendly, admitting your own mistakes, helping others to express their feelings.

It helps to understand that groups go through a process of development from early days where individuals are unsure or reticent, through a stormy time when there may be conflicting priorities or preferences until the goals become more clear and relationships become established, and then to a fruitful period when members trust each other and work together well. Discussing and clarifying goals, roles, procedures and relationships help ease the group into productivity.

Where a group has the following:

- a clear purpose
- a commitment by all to that purpose
- a common and inspirational vision
- explicit values

- clear roles and commitments
- active work to be done
- a group identity
- an ability to handle conflict
- a recognition of its own worth

then great things are possible – the skills, knowledge and experience of all members can be tapped – the group can work together productively and harmoniously. Time is well spent in establishing the task *and* process of a new group, or reviewing the operation of an existing group. A Facilitator can help a group to achieve its goals, manage periods of change and work together more harmoniously by guiding the process – by actively nurturing the conditions in which the group will flourish.

Experience in the Facilitator role and practice of facilitation skills do not necessarily transform the person into a skilful practitioner. However, being able to reflect on performance and events honestly and with insight, and learning from that process of reflection, help to effect the transition.

The knowledge and skills of the Facilitator can be acquired by many of us with study, practice and reflection. The process takes time. Personal qualities and individual style play a significant part and no two Facilitators operate in exactly the same way. You may wish to refer to Duffy and Griffin (1999) if you are unfamiliar with any of the concepts summarised in this chapter.

Chapter 2

Introduction to this volume

Summary

In this chapter we outline the structure of the book and explain how its content is organised into:

- *theory*
- *reference to general practice*
- *case studies from local projects where facilitation was a key change agent*
- *suggestions for facilitating change within your own practice or group*
- *tips and tools to help you facilitate.*

We set the scene for the practical advice that we offer subsequently on managing organisational change, by looking at some aspects of organisational structure and culture which can affect the relationship between the individual and the organisation.

The handbook is divided into three main sections, entitled:

- Introducing a change
- Features of organisations
- Instigating a programme of planned organisational change.

There is also a summary chapter entitled 'The Facilitator as change agent'.

In each of the three main sections you will find:

Theory

A brief overview of some of the relevant body of knowledge about managing change within organisations.

General Practice

How theory translates to real life in general practice.

Case Study

An example from general practice.

Tips and Tools

For diagnosing organisations, planning and managing change, reviewing progress – all tried and tested in the context of general practice.

Facilitate Your Own Practice

How you can help the process of managing change in primary care.

Setting the scene

In volume 1 (Duffy and Griffin, 1999) we focused on the 'individual in the group' and 'the group' *per se* and how we might facilitate groups, employing our own facilitative skills and behaviours and using tools and interventions, without being much concerned about the wider context within which groups operate.

For facilitation of short-life groups or specific situations we might 'get away' with not knowing much about the wider context, but if we want to facilitate longer-life groups effectively, we must be able to conduct a deeper analysis into why individuals and groups behave as they do, taking cognisance of both the organisational structure and culture, since both of these affect behaviour.

Sociologists have long argued that people's attitudes are shaped *as much* by the organisations in which they work as by their personality variables which they bring to the organisation. For example, the constraints and demands of the job can dictate their behaviour.

We need to think, therefore, about two key concepts at this stage – *structure* and *culture*.

The **structure** of organisations is something that may be reasonably straight-forward to grasp. For most large organisations in this century the usual structure is pyramidal, i.e. Chief Executive at the top, down through the senior management levels to the 'workers' at the bottom. We can see this in the typical health board or trust-type structures, where authority and power are largely linked to position in the hierarchy and there are clear lines of accountability drawn between the different hierarchical levels.

The majority of employees are nearer the bottom levels and are largely responsible for providing the service or manufacturing the product. There are formal systems, and task and reporting relationships, which function to co-ordinate, motivate and control employees so that they work together to achieve the goals of the organisation.

Smaller organisations, e.g. a general practice, might have a 'flatter' structure and be less hierarchical. There may not be one person at the top with ultimate authority and accountability, and the number of levels of line management are much fewer, and in our experience may be blurred! Power (or lack of it) can be linked to individuals' personalities (i.e. personal power) rather than to positional power *per se*.

Culture

Culture, however, is a harder term to grasp. The concept of culture is a controversial subject at a theoretical level, with the literature full of models and various theories, many of them inconsistent with each other. The following might be a working definition.

> **Culture is . . .**
> *The collection of beliefs, values, attitudes; customs, traditions and practices (the 'norms'), which are shared by an organisation's members and which are transmitted from one generation of employees to the next.*
> (after Buchanan and Huczynski, 1997, p. 512)

New employees are inducted into the culture through various formal and informal methods, such as joining regular meetings, attending orientation courses and engaging in social events. They may absorb certain other cultural elements through observing the type of language used and the physical layout of the building.

It can take a long while to grasp the organisation's culture and to begin to understand why the organisation, and the groups and individuals within it, may act as they do. People moving across organisations often talk of experiencing a 'culture shock'.

It can also become very uncomfortable for people who work in organisations whose cultural beliefs and values, for example, conflict with their own. Discomfort also follows if their personal expectations or goals are not being met, for whatever reason (e.g. expectation of rewards such as promotion, recognition, respect).

These discomforts can overspill into their groupwork and interactions and result in non-facilitative behaviours, such as lack of commitment, withdrawal, dismissal, blocking.

As Facilitators we need to be aware of how cultural factors may be affecting participation, commitment, willingness to change and coping ability – particularly when facilitating change.

You may be familiar with the theories of Abraham Maslow (a humanistic psychologist) in this context:

- **'self actualisation'** (Maslow, 1954) – all human beings have vast resources for healthy and successful living, which require the right social and organisational cultures for optimal growth and development
- and **'motivation'** – the internal psychological process of initiating, energising, directing and maintaining goal-directed behaviour.

Maslow argues that we have nine innate needs, which can be organised into a loose 'needs hierarchy'. A need is not an effective motivator or driver unless the needs lower in the hierarchy are largely satisfied. Additionally, we have an innate desire to 'work our way up' the hierarchy, pursuing the satisfaction of higher-order needs once our basic, lower-order needs are satisfied.

1 *Biological needs*	For example warmth, food, water, oxygen: basic to our individual and collective survival
2 *Safety needs*	For example security, comfort, shelter, freedom from fear, order, tranquillity
3 *Affiliation needs*	For example attachment, affection, giving and receiving love, relationships
4 *Esteem needs*	For example confidence, independence, prestige, achievement
5 *Need to know and understand*	For example learning, exploring, experimenting, curiosity
6 *Aesthetic needs*	For example order and beauty
7 *Self-actualisation needs*	For example development of our capabilities and potential to their fullest
8 *Transcendence*	For example a spiritual need – to be at one with the universe

The ninth need is that of *freedom of enquiry and expression*. Maslow argued that this was an essential prerequisite for the satisfaction of all the other needs. This is a significant need, both in the wider cultural context (i.e. differences between countries in the freedoms they allow individual citizens) but also in the organisational context, where free enquiry and expression are frequently constrained by procedures, rules, position and social norms.

Maslow's ideas have been criticised for being too *idealistic* – they present a typical picture of what might happen under ideal (and therefore rarely attained) social and organisational conditions; or too *vague* – are the higher-order needs (beyond biological and safety) really innate or are they learnt? Even with the help of his theory, behaviour may still be difficult to predict – fulfilment of satisfaction would measure differently for different individuals and therefore progress between one step and another would be difficult to define and measure. However, those of us working with groups seem to find some *face validity* in Maslow's theory, i.e. it feels right. There is no point striving to help a group to reach a valid consensus, if, for example, they're all cold and hungry, as they will not concentrate properly! How can there be open communication in a group if the organisational culture promotes blame, secrecy or partisanship?

Some other concepts in respect of the individual which are important in providing insight into behaviour in groups or organisations, especially in relation to change processes, are:

- psychological success
- locus of control
- life cycles.

Psychological success

Argyris (1964) claims that psychological success is vital to the healthy survival and growth of a positive self-concept. Such success supports our feelings of competence and self-confidence in relation to those areas of our lives into which we put our energies and efforts. *Change, especially where this is externally imposed, can pose threats to our psychological success and subsequently to our self-concept.*

At such times, the change process needs to be managed skilfully and sensitively, so that threats to psychological success are minimised, and individuals are supported in the change, so that they are helped to:

- understand the challenges inherent in change and the nature of the expected change

- develop personal goals for the change process
- determine their own ways of reaching these goals and producing the desired end results
- assimilate and incorporate new elements into their self-concept.

Locus of control

Rotter (1966) proposed that it is possible to distinguish two types of individual control dynamics:

1 people may be identified as *'internals'*, in that their locus of control is within themselves, i.e. they feel very much in charge of themselves and recognise that they are in control of their own destinies

2 or they may be classed as *'externals'*, in that they perceive their locus of control is external to themselves, i.e. they feel they have very little control over what happens to them.

Work carried out by Phares (1976) clearly shows that individuals with an 'internal' dynamic are better able to make life choices, take responsibility for their own actions and the resulting consequences. They are also better able to cope with failure and learn effectively from failure. According to Phares, 'internals':

- have greater self-control
- are better at retaining information
- ask more questions of people, notice more what is happening about them
- are less coercive when given power
- see other people as being responsible for themselves
- prefer activities requiring skill to those involving chance
- have higher academic achievements
- are more likely to delay gratification
- accept more responsibility for their own behaviour
- have more realistic reactions to their own successes and failures
- are less anxious
- exhibit less pathological behaviour.

Research work in this subject area has very clear implications for organisations that wish their employees to work more creatively and co-operatively to the benefit of both themselves and the organisation as a whole. There is a need to identify and create an 'internal' dynamic both within the various organisational groupings and within the management culture itself.

Life cycles

An effective Facilitator is one who, during the process of promoting and supporting professional change, is also able to recognise and understand the complex processes of personal adaptation that will almost certainly accompany it.

Organisational and professional change is now a common and constant feature of our lives. These changes are superimposed on the personal lives we all lead, with their accompanying dimensions of relationships, ageing, responsibilities, health variations and the myriad of emotions that permeate our personal journey through life. Our personal lives are characterised by a struggle to survive and find fulfilment (Erikson, 1977).

The ways in which individuals behave in organisations and react to new changes and increasing expectations may be determined *as much* by their personal lives as by the specific details of the organisational issues of the day. Quite simply, their capacity to cope with organisational change will not be constant, but will be linked to the stage of their life cycle and the particular pressures under which they are currently living.

Theories of culture

The theoretical concept of culture is controversial, widely debated and there exists a large body of literature defining and explaining culture from multiple perspectives.

There are two main theoretical approaches to the concept of culture.

1 **Culture is a variable** – culture is something that an organisation **has**. This perspective sees culture as serving four functions:
    * providing a sense of identity for employees, increasing their commitment to the company, making their work more intrinsically rewarding and making them identify more closely with fellow workers
    * allowing employees to 'make sense of' what goes on around them, enabling them to interpret the meaning of different organisational events
    * helping to reinforce the values of the organisation; that is, of senior management
    * serving as a control device for management with which to shape employee behaviour.
                                    (after Buchanan and Huczynski, 1997, p. 515)
2 **Organisations *are* cultures** – culture does not exist independently from people, but is constructed by company employees as they interact with one another on a daily basis.

Culture is seen as existing in, and through, the social action of cultural members, acknowledging the possible existence of several competing cultures within a single organisation, e.g. between different departments or functions. It is also recognised that there is a difference between the culture of non-management groups and that espoused by management, and that there are problems in aligning these to create a unified culture.

In examining an organisation's culture, we examine the beliefs and values that guide organisational members when they are participating in organisational activities, and how these are established, communicated and influenced.

Morgan (1997) suggests that 'one of the easiest ways of appreciating the nature of corporate culture and subculture is to simply observe the day-to-day functioning of a group or organisation to which one belongs as if one were an outsider' (anthropological stance). 'The characteristics of the culture being observed will gradually become evident as one becomes aware of the patterns of interaction between individuals, the language that is used, the images and themes explored in conversation and the various rituals of daily routine.'

Handy (1993) offers a view on culture which classifies it into four main types, each reflected in a structure and a set of systems: *power*, *role*, *task* and *person* cultures. He emphasises that each can be a good and effective culture, but that people are often 'culturally blinkered', assuming that ways which work well in one place can be successful elsewhere, whereas this is not always the case. His thesis is that structures reflect cultures – that the ills of organisations stem from imposing an inappropriate structure on a particular culture, or from expecting a certain culture to thrive in an inappropriate climate.

In the FED project conducted by Duffy, Griffin and Bain (Duffy *et al.*, 1998), the Facilitators worked hard, through observation and interpretation, to try to appreciate and understand the nature of the culture in the various practices in which they worked. They encountered a number of practices where the effect of the leadership style was to create a superficial appearance of harmony while driving conflict underground, leading to situations where the practice was increasingly unable to deal with real problems. With the management style effectively preventing the discussion of differences, genuine concerns were not given the attention they deserved, and development was slow, if not impossible.

We can now begin to appreciate the potential influence of both organisational structure and organisational culture when working with groups. Experience of external Facilitators points to there being multiple possible forms of general practice culture even where the structure is broadly similar. 'Getting a handle on the culture' is therefore a key competence which a Facilitator must develop. It becomes particularly important when working with a general practice over the medium to long term. The impact of the culture on the individuals in the group may be expressed in their level of participation, willingness to express feelings or concerns, ability to cope with the demands of change, or commitment to implement any new systems or procedures agreed by the group. If the Facilitator can become skilled in diagnosing the practice culture, it will help her in the planning, scheduling, supporting and reviewing of any facilitated change process. We will describe in Chapter 5 a practice characterisation model that can aid practice diagnosis.

Chapter 3

Introducing change

Summary

In this chapter we look at the conditions conducive to bringing about change and the problems typically associated with failure to implement change.

We describe the ongoing climate of change in general practice and some of the reasons why general practitioners have resisted imposed changes. Practice-based audit is suggested as a technique for encouraging ownership of change. The role of facilitation in audit and in other change processes is outlined.

In practical terms we suggest that you can facilitate change within your practice by:

- encouraging planning for change
- exploring worries about the impact of change
- diagnosing barriers to change
- dealing with conflict in a group
- encouraging collaboration in managing a change
- making progress with implementation of change
- identifying and agreeing responsibilities for implementing change.

We illustrate all these suggestions for facilitative actions with appropriate tools.

Theory

Bringing about change

Most organisations are continually changing, adapting and even transforming. The only constant is change. Organisational development is increasingly dependent on strategic planning, effective communication, collaboration between different specialties and clear lines of accountability. Teamwork, wider consultation within the workforce and broader participation within the management are seen as the way forward. This movement towards co-operation and individual responsibility creates a need for adjustment which some people find hard.

The common wisdom is that three ingredients are necessary to bring about any kind of change. These are:

1 **A dissatisfaction with the present situation**.
2 **A common vision of a more desirable future**.
3 **Knowing the first steps to take**.

However, if the current situation feels comfortable to some members of the organisation, change will be difficult to effect. Similarly, others may have come to tolerate a poor situation from force of habit and on balance opt to retain it rather than face the upheaval of change.

Additionally, commitment to change may be hard to achieve if there is no clear vision about the probable outcome of any change or if the clearly viewed outcome is not seen as desirable. More problematically, the first step may not be obvious or may seem impossible to achieve.

When there *is* dissatisfaction with the present situation, and there *does exist* a common vision of a more desirable future – and the organisation or group *does know* how to take the first steps – the group can weigh up any proposed change against predicted costs or implications of that change. If the potential benefits of the proposed change seem to outweigh the predicted costs, then the change is likely to go ahead.

Research shows that people will accept change if:

- they can see some advantage to themselves in doing so
- the change is compatible with what currently happens
- it is not too complex
- it can be adopted gradually
- they can see that it works.

Nevertheless, there are still problems in implementing change even when the change is seen to be acceptable.

Problems in implementing change

Woodcock and Francis (1981) identified eight sources of problems in successfully implementing change in organisations:

1 unclear aims of the organisation
2 ineffective leadership
3 unassertive management
4 negative climate
5 inappropriate structure
6 unbalanced power relationships
7 undeveloped individuals
8 ineffective teamwork.

Problems can also occur when the overall strategy used to manage the change fits poorly with the prevailing culture. Here is what happened when an external practice development Facilitator was invited into the Rose Practice to help them construct their practice development plan.

Case Study 1
The culture of the Rose Practice

A practice development facilitator had a preliminary meeting with the senior partner and practice manager of the Rose Practice – a large rural practice with six partners and a patient population of 9000 patients. She learned that the practice had had an 'away-day', out of which had emerged a set of broad goals for the development of the practice. What was now required was to detail the actions, the people involved and the timescale – so that these goals could be achieved.

The senior partner made known his commitment to teamwork, to valuing contributions from all staff and to being flexible in the face of change. The practice manager said very little. It was agreed that the whole practice team would divide into four multi-disciplinary groups which would meet and each work on two of the agreed goals, so that a working group comprising representatives from each of the small groups could come together at a later date and put together a draft action plan.

The Facilitator offered to work with the small groups, but that offer was declined. The GP did agree, however, that she might send a help sheet to guide each of the groups. The practice manager insisted on allocating members to the groups as she knew certain people 'would not work well together'.

Here is the advice the Facilitator sent:

Staff group planning session

Members to attend: all those listed in your particular group

Venue and time: suitable to the individuals concerned but before 25 September

General aim: to make specific proposals for action to a representative working party of the practice team, based on the agreed practice development goals

Objectives:

1   to discuss in depth the two broad goals attached
2   to detail specific objectives based on each of these goals, so that the goals can be achieved
3   to determine who will do what and when
4   to agree a final list of detailed proposals to be taken to the working party on 28 September
5   to appoint a spokesperson for your group.

Some general tips for more effective group working:

1   Agree on procedures before you start discussion – what time you will start and finish, who will take notes, who will represent the group at the working party, how you will all contribute, what type of behaviour will be useful (*see below!).
2   Ensure that everyone understands the purpose of the meeting and the need to generate as many and as varied ideas as possible. Then direct all energies to achieving your aims – don't use this session to exchange information that does not contribute directly to decision making.
3   Stick to areas where the group has a real contribution to make to the practice in terms of knowledge or relevance to their work.
4   Be specific in proposals, e.g. *not* 'improve communication in the practice' *but* 'identify what specific clinical information is required by each member of the team in order to function effectively'.
5   Generate ideas freely, e.g. brainstorm. Check that everyone is clear what is being suggested in each case. Then discuss the potential benefits and possible costs of such action.
6   Establish some criteria for evaluating your proposals, e.g. *can be achieved with existing staff, can be achieved this year, will benefit patients*, etc., etc. – you know best here.

7 Evaluate all proposals based on your own criteria and seek agreement from all your group on the final list.
8 Recap on the decisions made and establish how your representative will take the ideas to the working party.

*Helpful behaviour	Avoid
Defining problems	Rejecting ideas without due consideration
Asking for and giving facts, ideas and opinions	Going off at tangents
Asking for and making suggestions	Attention seeking
Asking for and giving clarification, elaboration	Bringing in personal problems or irrelevant personal experience
Summarising discussion and progress	Showing indifference
Proposing new approaches and plans	Showing off
	Monopolising the discussion
Co-ordinating activities	Being aggressive
Maintaining the momentum	Day dreaming
Being friendly	Feigning agreement then complaining after the meeting
Showing warmth	
Encouraging	
Praising	
Inviting contributions from quiet members	
Expressing standards	
Describing reactions	

The Facilitator was surprised when she attended the working group meeting to discover that one of the small groups had never even met, two of the small groups had failed to produce a written record of any decisions made, and that the senior partner had taken it upon himself to complete draft action plans for all the groups.

In the course of further involvement with the practice, the Facilitator came to understand that the key elements of the practice culture were, in fact, that:

- the senior partner usually acted in a dictatorial manner
- his values-in-action were quite different from his espoused values (i.e. he did not practise what he preached)
- the practice manager had grown weary of trying to effect a change to a more team-based culture
- the other partners had found their efforts to change a long-established hierarchical organisation fruitless, and so harboured much resentment
- the community nursing staff, located in a separate building, maintained only minimal functional contact with the practice
- the different staff groups generally had no history of working together in a truly multi-disciplinary way.

With hindsight, the Facilitator realised that the proposed strategy for managing the practice development process – and the one she would have favoured herself – was at odds with the existing culture. People in the practice expected to be *told* what was going to happen; there was no forum for discussing and sharing feelings and reactions; the senior partner made almost all the key decisions, largely without consultation. To achieve a modern, team-based, collaborative approach would have required a huge shift in attitudes, values and norms of behaviour in the practice.

Work with this practice, and many others in the region, provided a wealth of experience and evidence on which to base the subsequent construction of a Practice Characterisation Model, which would be used later as an aid to diagnosing any practice's ability and readiness to engage in systematic team-based development (*see* Chapter 5 for more details).

Strategies for managing change

Elizabeth Chell (1993) outlines three different strategies for managing change within an organisation.

- **Strategy one** assumes people are rational and motivated by self-interest. They only change when they come to realise that change is advantageous to them. The key tasks in managing or facilitating the change are in encouraging the group to fully explore the nature of the change, air any concerns, address any perceived problems associated with implementation and tailor the change process to achieve maximum possible benefit for themselves.

- **Strategy two** recognises that norms underpin behaviour – norms being imbued with feelings, beliefs, attitudes and values. Change will only occur if and when old norms disappear and are supplanted by new and appropriate norms. Energy and effort have to be put into dealing with feelings, mapping elements of the change on to existing beliefs and values, or encouraging a shift in attitude through clear explanation and new information which can alter priorities, or through incentives which are value based.
- **Strategy three** is based on the belief that change will only occur through the compliance of those with less power to those with more power. The management focus here will be more on clarifying responsibilities, detailing tasks and imposing penalties for non-co-operation.

You may want to give some thought to which strategy your practice tends to favour and whether or not it is appropriate in your particular situation.

Certainly, change seems to need positive and sustained effort. Many of us resist it because *it is personally challenging*:

- we would rather not face the problems of the existing situation
- it is not felt to be our responsibility
- we don't share with our colleagues a view of where we are all moving
- we don't feel confident about taking risks or we feel we haven't been consulted
- we feel the anxiety of loss of the familiar and the anxiety of the new.

Let's go on to look at how general practice has experienced change in recent years.

General Practice

A climate of ongoing change

From the introduction of the 1990 contract onwards, practices have felt that much change has been imposed from outside, particularly as a result of government directives. Scott and Marinker (1993), in the BMJ publication *Change and Teamwork in Primary Care*, remind us, however, that in *most cases* the reasons for change in general practice can be seen to be part of the natural development of the practice. Perhaps the proportion of elderly people in the local patient population has increased; there may be major staff changes – partners retire or new managers are appointed; the practice may become a training or research practice. These changes may present considerable challenges, but they will not be viewed as arbitrary impositions.

Reactions to change

When change is demanded by others and not seen to be on the basis of need, it does engender feelings of helplessness, hopelessness and general negativity. Change seems to be **arbitrary** when the initiator is strong and the evidence of need for change is weak. There is also a sense that **fashion** has played an important role in the development of latter-day general practice – we are familiar with the buzzwords which have migrated from industry through the educational sphere into general practice, such as *benchmarking*, *audit*, *performance review*, *appraisal* and *organisational development*.

Where fashions and trends have enhanced the quality and efficient delivery of services to patients, changes and change processes have been accepted and incorporated into the culture of general practice. However, the result of feeling a sense of slavery to fashion may explain much of the resentment felt by some general practitioners to academic bodies such as the Royal College of General Practitioners (Scott and Marinker, 1993).

They make the following points:

- change necessitated by circumstances is acceptable in general practice
- change willed and enforced by others is considered arbitrary
- often evidence is not available for required change
- change based on fashion is less acceptable than that based on sound evidence
- imposed change is more acceptable if it is expressed in terms of outcome rather than detailed behaviour
- the positive way to deal with imposed change is to create a sense of ownership of the change within the practice.

Barriers to building a shared commitment to change

A change-management course designed in the Grampian region of Scotland, and run by the Community Nurse Development Programme (Savage Young and Associates, describes some common barriers to building shared commitment to change.

Denial	Refusal to accept information or evidence because it is personally threatening
Blind spots	Failure to appreciate what is really going on; selective attention; being dishonest with oneself
Avoidance	Unwillingness to discuss issues because they would be hurtful or embarrassing or upsetting to talk about
Projection	Accepting the information but not responsibility for action
Lack of readiness	The need for change is accepted but the practice culture does not support or encourage new behaviour. There is lack of trust, poor teamworking, failure to share information appropriately, unresolved conflict
No shared model for change management	The practice has no established procedures or techniques for establishing where they are and where they want to go, and how they will get there
Change is perceived as arbitrary	There are no sanctions for failure nor rewards for success nor opportunities for choice
Overemphasis of rationality	Too much time given to the logic and the intellectual aspects, at the expense of the people issues

Audit as a change-management technique

Practice-based audit is one technique for encouraging ownership of, and commitment to, change in general practice. The original concept may have been 'fashionable' but grass-roots support and advice from audit facilitators' support groups have helped practices incorporate audit activities into their everyday life – you may remember 'Sally' from the first volume, a practice audit co-ordinator. Sally acknowledged the invaluable help of the Health Board Audit Facilitator who worked as both director, guide and support to the practice audit co-ordinators in the process of developing audit, and interpersonal and communication skills. Sally's view was that the help of the Facilitator had been the key to her progress so far. This facilitation model has been used effectively to integrate audit into practice life in more than 40 Tayside practices (Grant *et al.*, 1998). Its ultimate success will be measured by the extent to which the practice audit co-ordinators can fully facilitate and co-ordinate audit projects within their own practices.

Crombie *et al.* (1993) describe the essential features and principles of good audit:

- the primary aim is to improve the delivery of healthcare – effecting change should be the intention, observation *per se* may be interesting but leads nowhere
- the identity of staff and patients must be kept confidential
- the audit should be conducted in a supportive rather than judgemental environment; the conduct of audit studies often has a general educational benefit within a practice
- the audit should concentrate on topics that will lead to the greatest potential improvements in healthcare
- the methods used should be the simplest feasible to achieve the objective
- the key to effective audit is to determine the underlying cause of any deficiency in healthcare; a specific solution can then be devised
- audit studies must be flexible, collaborative and resourced
- effecting change is the most difficult stage of audit and should be handled with sensitivity and ingenuity
- the impact of any intervention must be assessed.

Set up and performed according to these principles, any practice-based audit is likely to effect change in the delivery of healthcare because it will:

- have been based on the local situation
- contain feedback on current practice
- have involved staff at all stages.

The role of facilitation in change processes

Facilitators have been used to train and support practice audit staff, and also to effect other changes in practices. This has been done through developing teamwork, aiding needs assessment, creating a climate of trust and confidence where barriers to change have been discussed and addressed, and also helping practices review the effects of changes made.

In the following case study, a health board Facilitator attended a practice meeting in a rural practice with a well-established primary healthcare team, to help the practice set their own priorities for action based on evidence that had been collected **by** the practice, **about** the practice, in a year-long needs assessment activity.

Case Study 2
The Tan Practice: determining priorities for change

The Tan Practice had collected a veritable mountain of information about its patient population, their health and social status, the range of services provided by the practice and the pattern of consultations, treatment and referrals. Now it was time to make some decisions about how to prioritise areas for action.

Each group within the practice had its own priorities – the practice manager, to cope with the demand for appointments; the practice nurses, to target more males in their health promotion activities; the community nurses, to deal with early discharges from hospital; the health visitors, to encourage responsible sexual behaviour among teenagers; the GPs, to provide more effective chronic disease management. How was the team to prioritise so that all would be committed to the development programme and all would feel that their views had been listened to and considered by the rest of the group?

A health board Facilitator proposed the use of **nominal group technique** (see p. 46). In this procedure representatives from the administrative, practice and community nursing staff groups joined the partners and the practice manager in presenting their individual top ten areas for action, explaining briefly the reasons for choosing them. The Facilitator listed all areas mentioned and, of course, there were many overlaps. A complete list of 28 areas was produced, all of equal priority at this stage. Each person then privately nominated his or her top five priorities, the results being collated by the Facilitator. Out of that group of 13 priorities, each then privately nominated his or her top three priorities. Finally, a list of eight priorities was agreed. These were:

* reduce smoking in the practice population
* identify undiagnosed mental health problems
* health promotion for teenagers
* greater understanding of others' roles in the primary care team
* more effective management of patients after myocardial infarct
* upgrade of practice premises to meet modern standards of service
* integration of practice and community nursing teams
* review of prescribing patterns within the partnership.

This technique helped to provide an opportunity for priority setting which was relatively free from the influence of status or power within the practice, was seen to be fair by all present and produced a working list of priorities to which all had contributed.

Facilitate Your Own Practice

Understanding (1) how people react to the idea of change, and (2) when change is likely to be implemented, is of help in facilitating change within your own practice.

In your role as an ordinary member of the team you may have little opportunity or power to influence, for example, the effectiveness of the leadership of your team or its unassertive management (unless of course you **are** the leader or the manager). However, on a basic level, you **can act** within groups to facilitate the process of working together better.

Encouraging	Being friendly, warm and responsive to others; giving others an opportunity to contribute or be recognised; accepting others and what they have to contribute
Harmonising	Reducing tension; helping others to express their feelings; trying to reconcile disagreements
Expressing group feelings	Sensing the mood of the group, the feelings and relationships within it; sharing your own feelings with the group
Gatekeeping	Helping to keep communication channels open; suggesting procedures that encourage participation
Compromising	Admitting your own mistakes; modifying your ideas in the interest of the group; offering a compromise even where it involves some loss of status
Standard setting and testing	Checking whether the group is satisfied with its own procedures; suggesting new procedures if necessary; monitoring that the group is maintaining standards

Formally facilitating change

In a more formal way there are a number of areas in which you can facilitate the successful planning, management and review of change processes.

You can:

- encourage planning for change
- explore worries about the impact of change
- diagnose barriers to change
- deal with conflict in a group
- encourage collaboration in managing a change
- make progress with implementation of change
- identify and agree responsibilities for implementing change.

Planning for change

When planning for change it helps if everyone shares a common understanding of exactly how the new situation will differ from the old and how that change impacts on them in their role in the practice. The tool entitled '**Paradigm shift**' (*see* p. 44) can promote shared understanding.

Very often when changes are introduced, or imposed, no one has looked systematically at the **impact of the change on individuals** in the setting. For example, when introducing a system of structured diabetes care into the practice, virtually everyone who works there will be affected in some way – GPs, the practice manager, the practice nurses, the reception and administrative staff, the community nurses (and of course, the patients). For each group/individual it is useful to identify:

- their present involvement
- the future expected benefit
- the potential costs
- their potential to wreck any planned change, through failure to co-operate in effecting the change.

Spiegal *et al.* (1992) have devised what they term a **domainal map** to identify just those issues. Figure 3.1 shows how a domainal map might look in a practice that is considering installing a computerised appointment system.

In the Tips and Tools section we describe these two tools: **paradigm shift** and the **domainal map.**

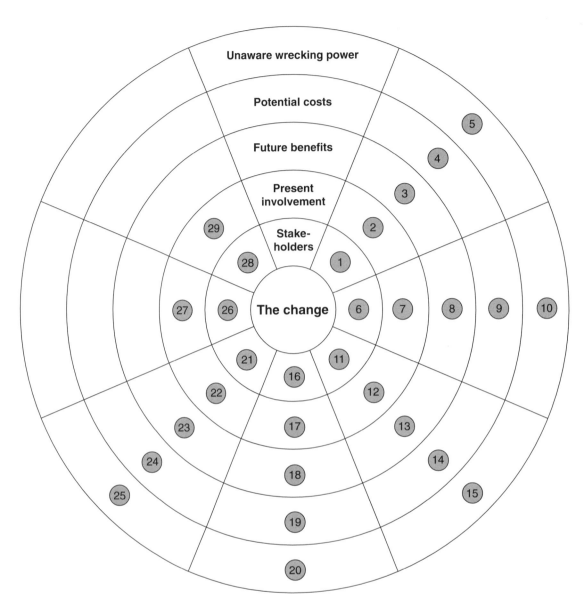

Figure 3.1 Domainal map.

Computerised appointment system

Stakeholders	Present involvement	Future benefits	Potential costs	Unaware wrecking power
① Receptionists	② Make appointments in two books	③ Increased flexibility when making appointments – by GP/by date/by time; surgery lists automatically generated	④ Training on new system; staff time away from practice; another terminal for reception	⑤ Some want to keep the manual system going as well, 'in case the computer crashes'
⑥ Practice secretary/audit co-ordinator	⑦ Audits appointments and produces report manually	⑧ Package produces appointment statistics automatically, less work/time involved; less margin for error?	⑨ Training on the new system	⑩ May feel her special expertise will no longer be required; how will she justify use of her time?
⑪ GPs	⑫ Not involved; all appointments made at reception	⑬ Could book repeat appointments before patient leaves consulting room; would know in advance which patient was coming and have computer medical record ready	⑭ Training requirement; more desk-top terminals required if all GPs are to conform	⑮ Some GPs not keen to change *status quo*; potential lack of compliance in use of the system
⑯ Practice manager	⑰ Not involved	⑱ More efficient use of her staff's time; better statistics available 'on demand', less pressure at reception	⑲ Financial aspects of system plus training costs	⑳ Finds introducing change difficult, lacks forward planning ability?
㉑ Practice nurse	㉒ Runs own manual appointments book, correlates own activity statistics	㉓ Would be able to book repeat appoint-ments before patient leaves consulting room; receptionists could deal with nurse's appointments	㉔ No terminal in practice nurse room; training costs	㉕ Is computer phobic and fears loss of autonomy over own area
㉖ Health visitors	㉗ Run own manual appointments book			
㉘ District nurses	㉙ Run own manual appointments book			

Exploring worries about the impact of change

Lack of information about what will be involved in implementing change, how to go about making the change and how to cope with the consequences all act as barriers to accepting the concept or complying with the new procedures or systems. You will find in the Tips and Tools section a description of a very simple discussion structure entitled '**Why worry?**' (*see* p. 52) to help pinpoint the worries of individuals about a proposed change.

Diagnosing barriers to change

In addition to '**Why worry**' you may also want to use '**Force field analysis**' (*see* p. 42) to identify barriers and their respective strengths so that a strategy can be devised to help overcome them.

Dealing with conflict in a group

Conflict is normal in any group. It can have the positive benefits of:

- challenging conventional wisdom, leading to innovation
- encouraging self-evaluation
- acting as an energising force to counteract staleness
- countering 'groupthink'
- improving the quality of decision making
- serving as an important 'release valve' to pent up personal or group tensions.

Change can create some anxiety in individuals and upheaval within the organisation which might generate conflict. The effects of the change for any individual might be perceived to be related to **territory**:

- *territorial violation* – if in one's job territory is either taken away or infringed upon; the practice manager having to hand over financial control to one of the partners, for example
- *overcrowding* (of roles or space) leading to frustration and energies devoted to protecting one's plot and if possible enlarging it – perhaps where the district nurse brings her expertise in dressing leg ulcers into the treatment room, the domain of the practice nurse

or to **values and roles**:

- *formal objectives begin to diverge* – one partner is focused on maximising income, while another is more committed to improving the practice's availability to patients

- *role definitions diverge*, e.g. the health visitor's understanding and expectation of having a largely autonomous professional role in the practice versus the GPs' expectation of her role and its limitations.

If conflict is not managed in its early stages, then what is likely to follow is:

- a 'hardening' of the conflict, so that it perpetuates itself as each tactic is met with other tactics
- the distortion and control of information, the checks and the barriers all working to promote hostility and suspicion
- collaboration degenerating into bargaining
- the misapplication of individual and group energies.

Within the practice, ensuring appropriate consultation, adhering to agreed ground rules which respect individuals, using suitable decision-making techniques and recording decisions in proper minutes can all help to prevent or manage conflict. Where formal facilitation to reconcile opposing views is required, Lois Hart (1992) suggests a six-step process, as described below.

Mediating conflict

Step 1 Suggest that the team use your presence as a third party to help in resolving a conflict. Get their commitment to proceed.

Step 2 Arrange that the two people in conflict sit facing each other and that you sit so that you can see their faces clearly.

Step 3 Ask one person to explain what the conflict is about and how they feel. The second person listens, and then is asked to paraphrase what was said. The second person then states what they think the problem is and how they feel. The first person listens, then is asked to paraphrase what was said.

Step 4 The first person now states the desired outcome. The second person then paraphrases it. The second person states the desired outcome and the first person paraphrases.

Step 5 This process of stating, listening and paraphrasing is continued with the goal of clarifying issues, hearing the desired outcome and finding a solution between the two people. When consensus is reached and both agree to a solution the process is complete.

Step 6 Together evaluate how this process worked and discuss with group members how it might be used in the future.

Encouraging collaboration in managing a change

With the increased emphasis on working in teams in general practice comes the need for collaboration in managing a change. Spiegal *et al.* (1992) developed a model using a team approach to managing change, which you might want to suggest as a strategy to be used by your group.

Encouraging collaboration in managing a change

1 Be explicit about why you think it is important to involve the team member.
2 Behave with trust towards your colleagues, expecting them to look at the idea objectively and not ridicule it.
3 Be receptive to both positive and negative responses to your ideas and be seen to value each person's opinion, even if it contradicts your original thinking. Agreement achieved after negative reactions have been identified and explored is more powerful than premature agreement obtained by evading potential conflict.
4 When potential benefits are identified, it is important that these should be seen as realistic and obtainable.
5 When team members identify the potential costs to themselves, these must be addressed, however trivial they may seem. Strategies for minimising such costs can then be explored. Team members will often need this opportunity to express and deal with the fear which may accompany proposals for change.

Making progress with the implementation of change

When your group is making unacceptably slow progress or is actually stuck, you might find it helpful to identify the forces that are driving the change and those that are opposing it, in order to take some action to produce movement. The technique known as **force field analysis** opens up a group's thinking and helps to produce creative solutions. It is described more fully at the end of this chapter (p. 42).

Identifying and agreeing responsibilities for implementing change

Successful implementation of change can be a problem when responsibilities, timescales and resources are not sufficiently specified at the planning stage. **Responsibility charts** encourage those who have decided on a particular change to think through the range of people who need to be involved and what their level of involvement would be. A case study from the Black Practice shows how it might work. A subgroup of this semi-rural, four-doctor practice was considering starting up a travel clinic.

Case Study 3
The Black Practice: Introducing a travel clinic

The practice nurses in the Black Practice decided at their monthly nurses' meeting that a travel clinic might be an effective way of providing systematic information and vaccination services to patients at a recognised time each week. The clinic would ensure that consistent advice and treatment was being provided, patients would know that there was a specific time and place to obtain the service, and it would allow the practice to plan more effectively for the ordering and storage of supplies.

As a first step, the nursing group looked at **who** in the practice would have to be involved in the setting up of such a clinic, so that they could ensure all relevant people were included in the discussions at an early stage. A blank chart is included on p. 47 (adapted from Mathew, 1994). Their **responsibility chart** looked like this:

Person	GPs	PM	CNs	PNs (AW, RM, KS)	Comp. operator	Recep.	Pharmacist	Patients
Decision								
Audit numbers using service last year	A	I/S	I	RM – R	R			
Define patients' needs	C	C		All – R		C	C	C
Devise protocol	C/A	I	I	All – R	I	I	C	
Decide timing of clinic	A/S	A/S	C	All – R	I	C	C	C
Advertise clinic	A/S	A/S	I	AW – R		I	I	I

R, responsible for making it happen; A, must approve; S, must support (devote resources); C, must be consulted; I, must be informed.

An **action plan** is a similar way of presenting an at-a-glance view of who needs to be involved in the successful implementation of any change. It should include a timetable for action and a requirement to review the change after a specified length of time. In the Tips and Tools section you will find a blank action planning sheet for you to copy and use (p. 50).

An action plan can help overcome the commonly reported difficulties practices face in seeing good ideas translated into manageable plans which can then be implemented and reviewed in a systematic way.

Here are some comments from practice members who were asked to comment on any action their practice may, or may not, have taken following detailed organisational diagnosis by an external Facilitator, followed by priority setting by the practice (Duffy *et al.*, 1998):

> '*We had lots of ideas but somehow they never came to fruition.*'
> '*We talked a lot but at the end of the day there was really nothing much down on paper and now most of us can hardly remember what was decided.*'
> '*We know broadly what has to be done here – but who is actually going to do it – and when?*'
> '*I think a number of changes have been made but I don't know the details of them or who has been involved.*'

Part of the key to planning and implementing change, however, is to run effective meetings. The process of designing an effective action plan requires a group to work in a structured and facilitative fashion. We devoted a whole chapter in volume 1 to improving meeting skills (Duffy and Griffin, 1999).

Below is an example of how the Azure Practice managed a review of their meetings with the help of the Facilitator. The Azure Practice was a small, family-centred practice in a busy suburb of a big city. It tended not to be particularly innovative or dynamic, but took pride in providing prompt appointments and a comprehensive type of family-based care, based on traditional values and commitment. However, members of the team recognised that their meetings tended to be disorganised, rambling and generally rather unproductive. Systematic planning for change was hard to achieve in this situation. An external Facilitator helped them to devise a programme for reviewing and improving the function and conduct of their practice meetings.

This practice subsequently went on to produce their practice development plan ahead of schedule and have retained their improved meetings as an integral part of the management of both clinical and organisational issues.

**Case Study 4
The Azure Practice:
Changing the function and conduct of practice meetings**

Action plan

Steps to take/ objectives:	Who will be involved?	Who else needs to know?	What is the timescale? (start date/ completion date/ongoing, etc.)	Who will review it and when?
Identify common problems with our meetings	Facilitator and whole practice team		Next whole-practice meeting	All – after 3 months
Run a training session in meeting skills	Facilitator and whole practice team		Within 1 month of first meeting	All – repeat if necessary after 3 months
Rectify administrative problems associated with the meetings procedure, as identified above	Chairman and practice manager	Whole practice team	Beginning with the first practice meeting following the training session	All immediately and again after 3 months
Develop appropriate interpersonal skills	Whole practice team	Facilitator	Ongoing	All – in 3 months
Develop decision-making skills	Whole practice team	Facilitator	Ongoing	All – in 3 months

In general, what we are suggesting is that you help your practice, either leading from the front or as an active enthusiastic team member, to think through any changes in a more systematic way – to plan, implement and review on a cyclical basis. You can effect this process by flagging up the importance of the cycle, and you may be in a position to suggest using some of the specific tools we go on to describe in this next Tips and Tools section.

This cyclical process becomes particularly important if a period of planned organisational change on a large scale is instigated. We will go on to look at that in Chapter 5.

> ## Tips and Tools

Change may be difficult to accept; change may be agreed but for some reason not effectively implemented; individuals and organisations may be unprepared for the knock-on effects of change. We have included in this section some tools which can help your group address these potential problems by including them at the planning stage. Your role may be to propose the use of these tools by whoever is 'in charge', or to facilitate their use. Your commitment to the process of groupworking will help your group take the time to make use of these tools, and later reflect on their value. The tools may then be incorporated into the practice culture if they are seen to be helpful.

Identifying what the change entails

'**Paradigm shift**' (*see* p. 44) asks participants in the situation to describe the current situation fully and then imagine the new situation. This shared understanding of the nature of the old and the new facilitates discussion on how to get from 'here' to 'there'. As an example, here is how a recent Facilitation Skills workshop (Duffy and Griffin, 1998) described the current situation in primary care and that which would be required under the Scottish White Paper *Designed to Care* (The Scottish Office, Department of Health, 1997).

Old paradigm	New paradigm
Competition	Collaboration
Continuing medical education	Continuing professional development
GP led	Team-based delivery of service
Practice-held data	Locality data sharing
Idiosyncratic IT systems	Locality health needs assessment
Practice-based organisation	Primary care trust
Variations in provision	Equality of access to services
Fundholding	Financial accountability
Clinical freedom	Clinical effectiveness measurement

Identifying the impact of the change on each individual involved

Very often when changes are introduced, or imposed, no one has looked systematically at the **impact of the change on individuals** in the setting. The domainal map of Spiegal *et al.* (1992) (p. 54) presents in a simple graphical way the answers to the following questions in relation to introducing a change into the practice:

1 What is the individual or group's current involvement in the area of the change?
2 What might the benefits of the change be to this individual or group?
3 What might the costs of this change be to this individual or group? (Such costs might include time, disruption, financial loss, training need.)
4 What power does this individual or group have to affect the successful implementation of this change?

We have included a blank domainal map at the end of this section (p. 54) with instructions for its use.

Examining a team's worry level about change

'**Why worry?**' (*see* p. 52) helps to pinpoint the worries of individuals about a proposed change as being related to **lack of information, effect on oneself, how to get it done** and **what might be the impact**. All members of the group think individually about their own worries and then discuss as a group the following questions (we use an example here of the introduction of a new computerised IT system for booking hospital appointments from the practice).

Why worry?

1 How do you feel about the forthcoming introduction of electronic hospital appointment booking?
2 Is there anything you question about this change?
3 What do you think will be the consequences of this change within the practice?
4 What are your doubts about this change?

Identifying barriers to change and encouraging progress

'**Force field analysis**' (*see* p. 42) can be used to stimulate action or enhance progress when you know where you want to go as a group but are either stuck or are making unacceptably slow progress. It does this by identifying forces driving and opposing the desired change and encouraging actions likely to produce some movement in the right direction. This technique opens up a group's thinking and helps to produce creative solutions. In brief, the technique asks the group to:

1 describe the situation before the change
2 agree the desired future state
3 brainstorm a list of forces which are pushing in the direction of the change and those opposing it
4 look at the restraining forces and see what can be done to reduce them
5 establish if action is needed to maintain the pushing forces
6 decide if some pushing forces can be introduced
7 assess whether there is a realistic chance of getting anywhere
8 if yes, plan who is going to do what, by when, etc.

Figure 3.2 gives an example of a force field analysis where the change in question is the introduction of a nurse triage system in a practice for handling patient telephone requests for home visits.

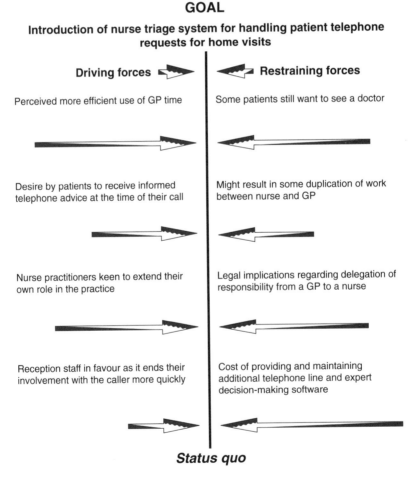

GOAL

Introduction of nurse triage system for handling patient telephone requests for home visits

Driving forces ➡️ ⬅️ **Restraining forces**

Perceived more efficient use of GP time | Some patients still want to see a doctor

Desire by patients to receive informed telephone advice at the time of their call | Might result in some duplication of work between nurse and GP

Nurse practitioners keen to extend their own role in the practice | Legal implications regarding delegation of responsibility from a GP to a nurse

Reception staff in favour as it ends their involvement with the caller more quickly | Cost of providing and maintaining additional telephone line and expert decision-making software

Status quo

Figure 3.2 Force field analysis – example 1.

Comprehensive instructions for use are included below. Some of these tools can be quite complicated at first glance. Before using them in their existing format, or in a format amended to suit your particular situation, you might want to consider the following guidance.

What is important when using tools is that:

- **you** understand how to use the tool
- **you** feel comfortable with the tool yourself
- you can **explain** to others the **benefits** of using a specific tool
- you can **allay any fears** about participating
- you can **give explicit instructions** to others
- you *and* they know that the **outcome** of the activity is intended to be.

And before using any **specific** tool ask yourself the following questions:

- What is the purpose of using this tool?
- What will be the potential cost in terms of time, effort and resources?
- Will this activity make good use of the group's time, effort and resources?
- Can every person in the group see its relevance and thus be committed to it?
- What are people's concerns about this activity? (Better to get these out into the open and address them.)
- What procedures have to be in place to carry out this activity?
- What will we do with the results?

Technique: **Force field analysis**

Purpose: • To stimulate action or enhance progress when you know where you want to go as a group but are either stuck or making unacceptably slow progress.
          • To identify forces driving and opposing the desired change and to take actions likely to produce some movement in the right direction.

Tips for use: Before discussing forces for and against, you need to establish a shared understanding within the group of the situation **now** and the **desired future state**. If these do not exist, use a brainstorming session or structured discussion to generate them.

          Keep the **now** and the **future** displayed in order to stimulate ideas.

          Brainstorm a list of forces which are pushing in the direction of the change or helping it in some way, and another list of those opposing it. These forces should be the ones applying to the group of people directly involved in managing the change (not necessarily the same group as the one doing the analysis).

          On the flipchart record the forces, their direction and relative strength (*see* Figure 3.3). When all ideas have been exhausted, you might want to use the following as a checklist to ensure that all possible ideas have been expressed:

          • personal
          • interpersonal
          • intergroup
          • managerial
          • organisational
          • technological
          • environmental.

          Then ask the following questions:

          • What can be done to reduce or redirect restraining forces without generating new opposing forces?
          • Is there any action necessary to maintain the pushing forces?

- Can some new pushing forces be introduced or existing ones strengthened without increasing resistance?
- Do you have all the information you need?
- Do you need to check out any of your assumptions?

Now assess if there is a realistic chance of getting anywhere. Is the desired state achievable? Do you have the option to modify the vision for the future?

If the decision is made to continue and a number of desirable actions have been identified, action plans ought to be devised so that the group knows who is going to do what, by when, etc.

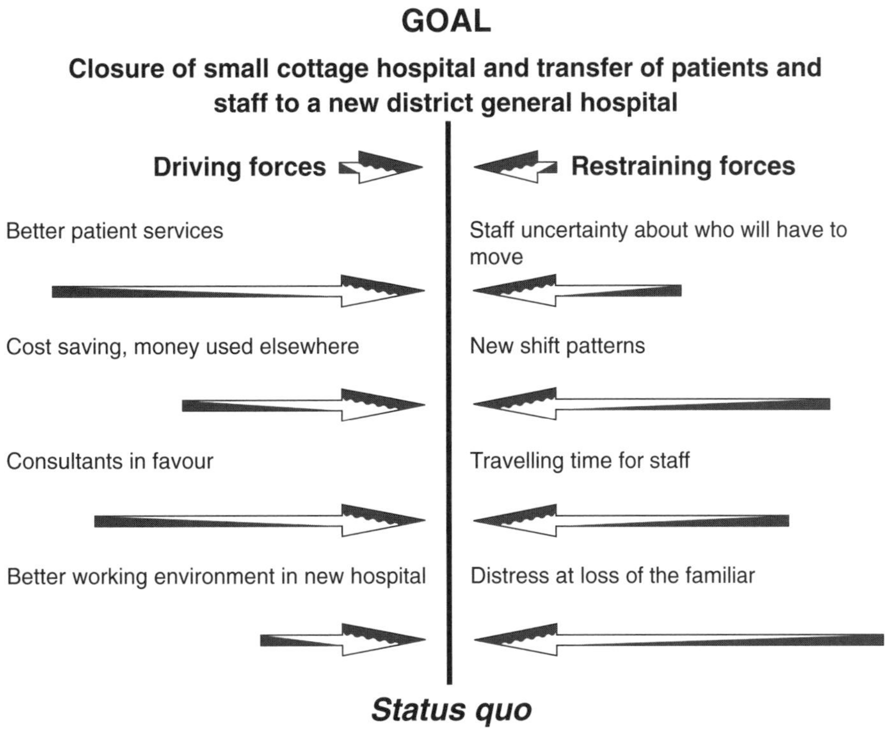

GOAL

Closure of small cottage hospital and transfer of patients and staff to a new district general hospital

Driving forces ▭▶   ◀▭ Restraining forces

Better patient services   Staff uncertainty about who will have to move

Cost saving, money used elsewhere   New shift patterns

Consultants in favour   Travelling time for staff

Better working environment in new hospital | Distress at loss of the familiar

Status quo

Figure 3.3 Force field analysis – example 2.

Technique:	**Paradigm shift** (adapted from Nilson, 1993)

Purpose: To clarify the minds of everyone in the group about the nature of the shift involved when a major change is to be instituted – the shift from the old way to the new way. It can be a useful exercise before beginning a discussion of organisational issues. Seeing the composite 'old' and the composite 'new' helps to reinforce the comparison and clarify the new way.

Tips for use: Prepare in advance a handout containing a list of terms describing the old way and the new way. Ask the participants to unscramble the terms, placing each in the appropriate column 'Old way' or 'New way'. This could be done in teams to stimulate some light-hearted competition. Note that some terms may apply to both old and new paradigms.

Use the completed correct lists to stimulate discussion. This could be done in conjunction with force field analysis (described above). An example is included below, where the new primary care-led NHS is compared to the old system.

Alternative: ask the group to identify the key features of both the old and the new – you may suggest some broad headings, such as:

- structure
- relationships
- systems and procedures
- groupwork processes
- technology
- environment.

Paradigm shift

Assign each term to the '*Old way*' **or** the '*New way*'

co-operation	competition
primary care trust	collaboration
continuing medical education	GP-led service
GP contract	quality measurements
idiosyncratic IT systems	health needs assessment
locality data sharing	clinical effectiveness measurement
financial accountability	practice-based organisation
continuing professional development	team-based delivery of service
variations in provision	primary care purchasing initiative
fundholding	equality of access
practice-held data	clinical freedom

Old way: fundholding, primary care purchasing initiative, practice-held data, clinical freedom, GP-led service, continuing medical education, idiosyncratic IT systems, practice-based organisation, competition, GP contract.

New way: equality of access, health needs assessment, continuing professional development, clinical effectiveness measurement, co-operation, collaboration, team-based delivery of service, locality data sharing, primary care trust.

Technique:	<h1>Nominal group technique</h1>

Purpose:
- To reach agreement on a list of priorities or key issues, giving equal weight to every participant's views.
- To identify all possible issues involved in a problematic situation.

Tips for use:

This is a useful technique where a group is composed of individuals of unequal status. All ideas are accepted in the first instance. All ideas are then clarified to allow shared understanding. Individuals then rank ideas according to agreed criteria. The final ranking is based on the collated results.

- Step 1: identify the question or problem, e.g. what are the main health needs of our patients?
- Step 2: using a round, ask each individual to suggest one item. Keep going until no new items are generated. Write each item on a flip chart.
- Step 3: clarify and confirm the wording of each item so that everyone is happy with that description. Then number each item.
- Step 4: depending on the length of the list, ask each member to select their ten top items without putting them in order. They can do this privately on paper.
- Step 5: collate all responses without identifying ownership.
- Step 6: re-order the list according to frequency of choice of specific items.
- Step 7: repeat the process if the list is still too long for your purposes. If the list is very long, you may need to select the top eight and then even the top five or three, dependent on how limited you want the final list to be.
- Step 8: your final list will reflect the relative importance of items to the whole group.

Variation: at step 4, ask group to *rank* top ten. Assign scores to each item. Agree collated scores will determine order.

Quick and dirty method: generate your list of items on the flip chart – either from a round or from summarising preceding discussion. Ask each individual to tick their top priorities on the chart itself. Can be done over coffee break. Offers less privacy.

Technique:

Responsibility charting
(adapted from Mathew, 1994)

Purpose: Successful implementation of change can be a problem when responsibilities, timescales and resources are not sufficiently specified at the planning stage. 'Responsibility charts' encourage those who have decided on a particular change to think through the range of people who need to be involved and what their level of involvement would be.

Person	GPs	PM	CNs	PNs	Comp. operator	Recep.	Pharmacist	Patients
Decision								

R, responsible for making it happen; A, must approve; S, must support (devote resources); C, must be consulted; I, must be informed.

Technique:	<div align="center">**Action planning**</div>
Purpose:	• An action plan is basically a road map for the management of a change.
	• It is **related** to the change goals and priorities.
	• It is **specific** in the way it details activities, timing and people involved.
	• It is **integrated** in that its parts are closely connected. And it is adaptable in the face of unexpected events.
Tips for use:	See below for an example of an action plan.

Formulate your **goal.** (Circumstances may have imposed the goal on you, or you may have decided on it yourselves as a group.)

Goals tend to be broad statements about the area you wish to develop or change, e.g. to review existing clinical management in the practice. They may focus on areas currently covered or on new areas.

Useful words for expressing goals might be:

• review
• introduce
• promote
• strengthen
• develop
• facilitate
• involve
• increase
• improve.

It is often useful to break goals down into more specific **objectives** which detail the specific action which needs to be taken to achieve the goal.

Good objectives are **SMART** (see tool on setting objectives, p. 120): Specific, Measurable, Attainable, Relevant, Timebound. Useful words for writing objectives are:

• define
• identify
• determine
• demonstrate
• record

- monitor
- assess
- construct
- list
- summarise.

Detail who will do what and when. It may also be useful to note who else needs to know, who will review it and when.

Revisit your action plan from time to time to see if it is still relevant and achievable.

Action plan

Overall development area: Clinical management.

Goal: To make audit an integral part of our management objectives.

Objectives:
1   Acquire sufficient skills to undertake audit as an integral part of the practice.
2   Allocate protected time for audit.
3   Implement data collection and retrieval systems that produce routine data for audit.

Objective 1: practice to acquire sufficient skills to undertake audit as an integral part of the practice's activities

What	Who	When
1 Identify the staff who need training	GPs/PM/Staff	May 2000
2 Identify the training they need	GPs/PM/Staff	June 2000
3 Identify sources of training	Practice manager	May–June 2000
4 Obtain resources required	Practice manager	July 2000
5 Make arrangements for training	Practice manager	August 2000
6 Trainees engage in training programme	Nominated audit trainees	2000–2001

Similarly, with objectives two and three, breaking each objective down into discrete steps.

Two action plan templates are given below.

Action plan		
Objective:		
What	Who	When
1		
2		
3		
4		
5		
6		

Action plan

Goal:

Steps to take/objectives	Who will be involved?	Who else needs to know?	What is the timescale?	Who will review it and when?

Technique: **Why worry?**

Purpose: This is a discussion format which helps to pinpoint the
                       worries of individuals about a proposed change as being
                       related to:

                       • lack of information
                       • effect on oneself
                       • how to get it done
                       • what might be the impact.

                       All members of the group think individually about their own
                       worries and then discuss as a group the questions below.

                       1   How do you feel about the forthcoming change in . . . ?
                       2   Is there anything you question about this change?
                       3   What do you think will be the consequences of this
                           change within the practice?
                       4   What are your doubts about this change?

Tips for use: Can be useful when a change is imposed from outside and
                       there is no option to reject the change. If the concerns
                       expressed are then addressed, individuals are more likely to
                       accept the change and comply with any requirements made
                       of them.

                       Discussion based around the questions may highlight
                       knowledge or skill gaps which training can help to fill. It
                       might also indicate areas for reorganisation to meet the
                       requirements of the proposed change, e.g. restructuring of
                       workload.

Materials   • A statement of the proposed change.
required: • A copy of the 'why worry' questions which focus on the
                         change.
                       • Post-its for individual ideas, concerns (optional).
                       • Flip chart to record main points of the discussion.
                       • Written record of any decisions made.

The Facilitator guides the process, encourages sharing of feelings and ideas
and records both the content and the outcome.

Technique: **Domainal map**

Purpose: Very often when changes are introduced, or imposed, no one has looked systematically at the **impact of the change on individuals** in the setting. For each group or individual it is useful to identify these issues:

- their present involvement
- the future expected benefit
- the potential costs
- their potential to wreck any planned change, through failure to co-operate in effecting the change.

This is a visual tool (developed by Spiegal *et al.*, 1992) which makes it easier to plan as a team how to implement decisions. The map is made up of six concentric circles, each representing one of the major issues listed above. Each circle is divided into a number of segments, each representing one group or individual who will be affected by a change – they are known as *stakeholders*. If these people are in favour of the change they can help promote it to others and effect successful implementation of it. If not, they may obstruct it. Similarly, if they have been consulted and are involved in negotiations and decision making, they are likely to be more committed to the change.

Tips for use:
1 Start with a blank domainal map (*see* Figure 3.4).
2 In the centre, fill in the title of the change you are planning to introduce or facilitate.
3 Move to the next band and fill in the names of the stakeholders who will be involved in the change.
4 In the next band, fill in the present involvement of each stakeholder (or group of stakeholders).
5 Move to the next band and fill in how the stakeholder(s) might benefit from the introduction of the change.
6 In the next band, note the potential cost to that stakeholder (or group) of implementation of the change.
7 Finally, in the outer band, note the ways in which each stakeholder (or group) could make it impossible for this change to happen (i.e. their potential wrecking power).

In this way, you have explored costs, benefits, implications and potential problems from a variety of viewpoints and are more likely to be in a suitable position to judge whether or not the change is feasible and manageable.

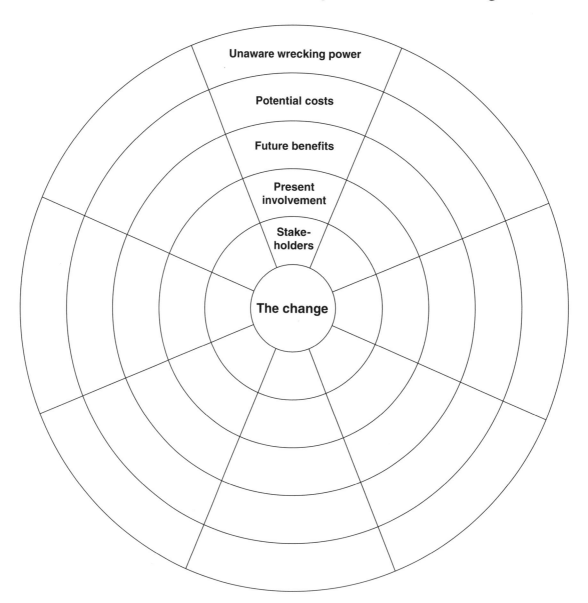

Figure 3.4 Blank domainal map.

Chapter 4

Features of organisations

Summary

In this chapter we describe some different ways of looking at organisations, using analogies or metaphors to aid understanding of what might be happening within general practice organisation.

We discuss how you can begin to characterise your own organisation, describing a diagnostic process which was used in Tayside to help practices to identify areas and priorities for development.

We suggest a number of techniques for reviewing communication, teamwork and overall effectiveness and efficiency within a practice.

Whatever your chosen option might be, we recommend that you think through the purpose, relevance, procedures, costs and benefits of engaging in any specific diagnostic process.

Theory

Ways of thinking about organisations

The study of people in organisations is not a modern phenomenon. For centuries, individuals (such as Confucius and Aristotle) have theorised and given insight into organising large numbers of people productively. However, in modern times, organisations have been studied and classified in a more systematic way. Gareth Morgan (1997) suggests that we tend to use **metaphors** and **analogies** to give us insight into, and understanding of, organisations. In other words, we use a way of thinking borrowed from another context to help us 'read' and understand what is happening in an organisation. This kind of thinking has relevance because organisations are complex and paradoxical phenomena.

Morgan suggests that we can think of organisations from a number of different perspectives, all having some validity.

- **Organisations as machines**, designed to achieve predetermined goals and objectives. The importance of human qualities is minimised. The organisation is expected to operate in a systematic, efficient, reliable and predictable way. The result can be lack of flexibility and adaptability in a changing world and a certain dehumanising experience for those working there.
- **Organisations as organisms**, where attention is focused on understanding organisational needs and environmental relations. Organisations are seen as being born, growing, developing, declining and dying. They are living systems which have to adapt to their environment. Employees are seen as having complex needs which have to be satisfied if they are to lead full and healthy lives and perform effectively in the workplace. The needs of individuals and the organisation must be integrated.
- **Organisations as brains**, where attention is centred on the importance of information processing, learning and intelligence, and to a set of design principles for enhancing these qualities so that the organisation can deal with the complexity and uncertainty presented by its environment. Innovative organisations must be learning organisations open to enquiry and self-criticism.
- **Organisations as cultures**, where the organisation is based on the ideas, values, norms, rituals and beliefs that sustain it as a socially constructed being. The truly human nature of organisations is recognised and with it the need to build the organisation around the people rather than techniques.
- **Organisations as political systems**, where the organisation is seen as a system of government, drawing on various political principles to justify different kinds of rules. Some may be highly authoritarian and others democracies – all are seeking ways to create order and direction among people with potentially different and conflicting interests.
- **Organisations as psychic prisons**, where people become trapped by their own thoughts, ideas and beliefs or by preoccupations originating in the unconscious mind. For example, members of an organisation may share illusions and standard ways of operating which interfere with their ability to think critically – a phenomenon known as 'groupthink'. In others, the

organisation of certain aspects of work may be in response to unconscious defences, e.g. treating the patient as a 'case' rather than a 'person', and so providing a defence against anxiety in the clinician dealing with distressing tasks.

- **Organisations as instruments of domination**, where they often use their employees, the community in which they operate and the world economy to achieve their own ends. The essence of organisation rests in a process of domination where certain people impose their will upon others.
- **Organisations as flux and transformation**, where organisations are self-producing systems which create themselves in their own image or, alternatively, are the products of circular flows of negative and positive feedback.

These are only ways of **thinking** about organisations but Handy (1993) would agree with Morgan in stating that the way you **think** governs the way you **act**. There is probably no one definitive view when you are trying to understand or deal with an organisation, but these multiple perspectives may help to give us insight when trying to 'diagnose' the organisation in order to predict events or influence the future.

General Practice

Diagnosis of the practice as an organisation

How do we begin to understand what is going on in any general practice organisation?

We can start from the premise, as Morgan (1997) does, that organisations can be many things at one and the same time, but recognise that his different perspectives can be used in a practical way to read and understand specific situations. It might then be possible to shape the management and design of the organisation.

General practice in the UK is designed in a somewhat **mechanistic** way to achieve certain goals – immunisation of all children against certain illnesses, for example. It is also an **organism** adapted to survive in certain environments and not others – it would not survive in its current form in the USA, for example, where the funding system is totally different. It is increasingly an **information-processing system,** tracking, for example, patients, conditions, treatments and outcomes. It is skilled in clinical **learning** but possibly not in collaboration. It has a defined **cultural identity**, which is characterised by distinctive beliefs and values (although these are not always made explicit). It does exhibit some **political** wrangling, e.g. over status and power within the new primary care-led system. Recent changes in its design and operation do **reflect changes** in social organisation and values, 'customer care' being one. **Feedback,** both positive and negative, from patients or from practice accreditation reviews do effect change in the shape of the organisation. Like other types of organisations, it does provide opportunities for some people to **dominate** others.

Organisational diagnosis to help identify priorities for development

A recent project (Duffy *et al.*, 1998), devised and carried out by a team from Tayside Centre for General Practice at the University of Dundee, attempted to use 'organisational diagnosis' to help 15 practices identify their own priorities for development and so begin a process of organisational change. This project recognised the interplay between information management, teamwork and clinical-service delivery in the functioning of practices. It therefore explored, in individual interviews with all members of the primary healthcare team:

- attitudes
- values
- roles
- expectations
- systems
- collaboration
- knowledge
- decision making
- IT skills
- training
- education.

All views were accorded equal weight, and common themes were presented and explored in a feedback report to the whole practice about the organisation of the practice.

The route of questioning is shown below. This was an outline guide for the interviewer to follow but could be varied, depending on the specific situation within any given practice.

Case Study 5
Diagnostic questions

1 What is it like to work here?
2 In your own words, could you say what this practice is about?
3 How well do people work together as a team in this practice?
4 Do you feel comfortable in your own role in the practice? Do other people understand your role?
5 How good is communication in this practice?
6 How are decisions taken? How are changes introduced? Are ideas taken on board?
7 How well does this practice keep up with workload and meet patient demand?
8 Systems. Is there room for improvement in these systems? What are the problem areas? What works really well? Why? Are things kept up to date? Who is responsible for keeping things up to date? What is done on the computer and what is done manually?
9 What role does the computer have in your own work?
10 Are you using it as efficiently as you might?
11 Do you see room for using it more?
12 How do you identify your continuing educational needs? What training have you had since joining the practice?
13 Do you feel your skills are fully utilised by the practice? Do your skills fully meet the needs of the job? Who identifies your training needs?
14 As a group of staff, what are your development needs?
15 As a practice, what are your development needs (clinical and organisational)? What are your reasons for citing these?
16 What encourages change in this practice? What inhibits it?
17 What do you understand by the term 'practice development plan' and how do you think it will benefit the practice?
18 What part do you hope to play in it?
19 Is there anything else you would like to add?

The 'story' of each practice, presented in the feedback report, varied considerably. In one practice, common values linked to providing a high-quality, family-oriented service emerged as a key factor in the organisation. In another, lack of up-to-date information technology was restricting the delivery of a service fully responsive to the needs of the patients.

Here is one example of the conclusions attached to a much longer feedback report – about the Crimson Practice. This was a long-established, inner-city practice with a high and stable proportion of patients with chronic social problems, a practice which tended to be overshadowed by the more dynamic practices in the city. The Crimson Practice worked to high standards but had failed to capitalise in the past on opportunities to modernise systems and increase computerisation.

Case Study 6
The Crimson Practice: feedback report

Conclusion to feedback report
There seem to be a number of key points which arose from the interviews and which have been detailed in this report:

- the practice is at a crossroads in its development
- there is currently an opportunity to plan future development in a systematic way
- a number of key requirements for successfully implementing change already exist in the practice
- it is vital to improve the management of information within the practice, particularly through increased use of computers
- this is a suitable time for the practice to use its proven teamworking skills to concentrate more on clinical service development.

Results of practice diagnosis in 15 practices in Tayside

So what was the diagnosis of general practice in those 15 practices? Although every practice was unique in its organisation, in Tayside we found many examples of what we called 'good practice', as well as some typical problems. When thinking about 'treatment', we identified many valuable practice resources which might aid practice development.

In the '**good practice**' category, several areas of organisation featured. These included:

- clear lines of communication
- effective management of change
- efficient systems – appointments, filing, record keeping, etc.
- developed teamwork.

Among the **problem areas** could be found:

- lack of a formal communication structure
- non-productive meetings
- poor definition and performance of roles

- absence of team culture
- dysfunctional partnership
- absence of information management strategy
- inefficient systems
- inadequate resources
- need for additional services.

However, there were many **resources** identified which would **aid development**. These included, in varying combinations in different practices:

- positive attitude to development
- comfortable working environment
- significant levels of job satisfaction
- effective management
- workable partnership
- positive qualities of staff
- efficient use of information technology.

In thinking about facilitating development within your own practice, we will look in the next section at ways of diagnosing your organisation and identifying areas for development or change.

Facilitate Your Own Practice

Diagnosing your own practice

In addition to our own diagnostic questioning route for in-depth interviews which can generate a **practice characterisation**, a number of other tools have been suggested for use in general practice to identify and characterise organisational features within practices.

We describe in the Tips and Tools section a variety of these tools, as follows.

Team diagnostic survey	To assess the effectiveness of teamworking
360° evaluation	To gather information from patients, colleagues and all practice staff on where the practice and individuals are performing well and where there may be room for improvement or further training and education
Communication audit	To review patterns of communication within the practice

If you were to facilitate the introduction and use of any diagnostic tools, we suggest that first you consider the following questions.

- What is the purpose of using this tool?
- What will be the potential cost in terms of time, effort and resources?
- Will this activity make good use of the practice's time, effort and resources?
- Can every person in the practice see its relevance and thus be committed to it?
- What are people's concerns about this activity? (Better to get these out into the open and address them.)
- What procedures will have to be in place to carry out the activity?
- What will you do with the results?

Diagnosing your practice is an essential first step towards instigating a programme of planned organisational change – the subject of Chapter 5.

Tips and Tools for Diagnosing Your Practice

The Practice Characterisation Model

The findings from the FED project (Duffy *et al.*, 1998) suggest that practices can be characterised along four dimensions, using a number of indicators. Such a characterisation may be a useful aid to thinking about whether a practice is ready and equipped to embark on a period of major change or whether some other action is more likely to be productive. The **dimensions** are: *organisational state, current coping ability, culture of change management* and *readiness to face the challenge of change (development status)*. Each **dimension** may take two or more **forms** (e.g. *stable* and *unstable* are forms of the *organisational state* dimension). Each **form** will have a number of **indicators,** which assist in making a diagnosis. We detail the dimensions, the forms and the indicators below.

Characterising your practice – dimensions, forms and indicators

Dimension	Possible forms	Examples of indicators
1 *Organisational state*	Stable	i No major change in key personnel imminent or current (typically practice manager, often a partner) ii Partnership workable iii Management functional iv Systems adequate v Resources dependable vi Reasonable level of morale generally
	Unstable	*Any of the following indicators:* i Major change in key personnel current or imminent ii Moving to new premises iii Major alteration to practice systems, e.g. whole new computer system about to be installed iv Dysfunctional partnership v Widespread lack of confidence in management
2 *Current ability to cope*[a]	Coping	i 'Reasonable' waiting times for appointments ii Job satisfaction possible for most people iii No obvious problem with patient complaints iv Effective communication between different clinical and admin. groups
	Exhibiting acute problems	i A major incident occurring in the practice creating a 'shock' effect *Or a combination of two or more of:* ii Widespread low morale iii High staff turnover iv Poor performance in key areas v Obvious painful interpersonal problems, particularly within workgroups
	Exhibiting chronic problems	i General lack of job satisfaction ii Low morale iii Unsuitable premises affecting motivation iv Long-standing partnership problems v Lack of key resources vi Past failures to address problems
3 *Culture of change management*	Proactive	i Systems already in place for consultation, discussion, decision making and implementation of change ii Positive attitude to new ideas iii Practice able to review its own performance iv Practice accustomed to looking ahead

Characterising your practice – dimensions, forms and indicators (continued)

Dimension	Possible forms	Examples of indicators
	Reactive	i Makes changes only in response to problems or directives ii Nursing staff play no part in management decision making iii Practice heavily focused on the day-to-day issues
4 *Development status*	Stuck	i Lack of 'motivator' in the practice ii No forum for all staff to express ideas iii Widespread complacency iv Relative isolation from proactive groups v Becalmed after major organisational changes have bedded in vi Tendency to be reactive rather than proactive
	Keen to develop but lacking skills	i Ineffective implementation of good ideas ii No established structure for planning systematically as a team iii Anxiety about producing a plan for development iv Can produce wealth of ideas and suggestions for development v Would benefit from external support and training vi Recognise the value of being proactive
	Poised for development	i Have an established system of consultation, discussion, decision making, implementation and review of progress ii Have experienced positive planned change iii Possess appropriate skills and qualities in key people to manage and sustain change (motivation, leadership, commitment, enthusiasm, etc.) iv Exhibit a cohesive partnership v Have in place clear lines of communication within the team vi Work within well-defined and understood roles vii Show strong and effective management viii Have a positive attitude to the challenge of change ix Would benefit from an external viewpoint

[a] This second dimension suggests three forms – *coping, exhibiting acute problems* and *exhibiting chronic problems* – which are not necessarily mutually exclusive, since, for example, practices can exhibit both acute and chronic problems simultaneously. Additionally, they might possess some chronic problems but still be coping.

In a typical scenario, a knowledgeable but neutral Facilitator or practice development consultant might be brought in to diagnose your practice by means of observation, interviewing of all practice staff and discussion based around a feedback report (as described above, pp. 59–60). However, you may, as a practice, be able to make some reasoned judgements about **your own** general organisational state by using the questions in Case Study 5 as a starting point for discussion in facilitated groups. Your role, depending on your position in the organisation and the influence you have as part of your remit, could be:

- to facilitate these groups
- to ascertain commonly held views
- to report back to the practice the general consensus of opinion about the topics covered in the questions – how it feels to work in the practice, what works well and what doesn't work so well, how people work together as a team, etc.

In addition to employing facilitation skills in these group meetings you need to pay attention to:

- how the whole concept is introduced to individuals in the practice
- to what extent anonymity of views is protected
- what the outcome of any discussions will be
- what the benefit to both the practice and individuals working in it is intended to be.

In this next case study we look at the Coral Practice, a suburban, family-oriented practice which had recently survived a major upheaval of two partners splitting off from the practice and forming their own breakaway practice in an adjacent part of town. The Coral Practice were keen to think about developing their practice so as to continue to provide a personal, caring service to those patients who had stayed with them, but also to develop a more up-to-date and comprehensive service in order to attract some new patients.

Case Study 7
The Coral Practice: diagnosing for practice development

Through observation and interviews with all members of staff using the diagnostic questionnaire in Case Study 5, the Facilitator was able to 'diagnose' the practice organisation of the Coral Practice as *stable*, *coping*, *reactive* and *keen*.

Dimension	Indicators identified in this practice	Possible forms	Diagnosis
Organisational state	1 No major change in key personnel imminent	Stable	→'Stable'
	2 Partnership workable		
	3 Reasonable level of morale	Unstable	
	4 Inadequate computer system[a]		
Current ability to cope	1 Job satisfaction for most people	Coping	→'Coping'
	2 No obvious patient complaints	Acute	
	3 Reasonable waiting times for appointments	Chronic	
Culture of change management	1 Practice heavily focused on day-to-day issues	Proactive	
	2 Nursing staff play no part in management decision making	Reactive	→'Reactive'
	3 Makes changes only in response to problems or directives		
Development status	1 No established structure for planning systematically as a team	Stuck	
	2 Anxiety about producing a development plan	Keen	→'Keen'
	3 Can produce ideas for development but lacking skills to implement them	Poised	

[a] A 'positive' diagnosis can still accommodate some negative indicators.

On the basis of the diagnosis, accepted by the practice, the Facilitator in this case worked with the practice to develop and improve their skills and procedures for:

- working as a team
- using information management better in order to meet practice needs
- improving the productivity and effectiveness of their meetings
- clarifying roles and responsibilities within the management structure.

Once these process skills were in place, the practice was far better equipped to think about and plan its long-term development.

A full description of how to apply the practice characterisation model is given at the end of this chapter.

The Team Diagnostic Survey

Pritchard and Pritchard (1994) have developed a practical workbook for primary healthcare teams which contains a number of activities for team discussion and learning. These cover:

- the nature and purpose of teamwork
- team diagnosis
- team goals and tasks
- roles within the team
- meetings, decisions, procedures and use of time
- team leadership
- new team members and how they fit in
- working in a team
- team dysfunction
- the world outside the team
- evaluation of teamwork
- the way forward.

Of particular relevance here is their **team diagnostic survey** which is completed by each member of the team. Subjects choose a response from a number of options, which best fits their experience of: knowledge of team goals, clarity of role, participation, decision making, managing conflict, availability of team members and mutual support. To give one example, in the area of **managing conflict** the options are:

1   *We assume it is best not to get too personal, so we let it pass and hope it will soon be forgotten. If feelings start to get heated, we try to cool things down by*

making the least of the disagreement (for example, 'there is no point in getting angry, so let's forget it').

2 *We often end the disagreement when someone takes charge and makes a decision, and it is not discussed further.*

3 *We try to come to an agreement somewhere between the two conflicting positions. In other words we compromise, so everyone gains a little and loses a little and so we end the disagreement.*

4 *We try to get the disagreeing parties together and let them talk through their points of view, until each can see some sense in the other's ideas. They we try to reach an agreement which makes sense to everyone.*

Examples . . . .

A nominated person collates all the responses on to a single sheet and lists the comments under each heading. The diagnosis is then discussed as a group, topic by topic, with particular attention paid to areas of teamwork that stand out as satisfactory and unsatisfactory so that the team can see what is going well, before facing up to areas of teamwork that fall short.

Please see the end of this chapter for items from the complete questionnaire with instructions for use.

A computerised tool for 360° feedback

Insight 360° is a newly developed, computerised **diagnostic tool** for primary healthcare team use (Griffin *et al.*, 2000). The application is based on questionnaires for completion by practice clinicians, members of managerial and administrative staff and patients. These questionnaires investigate perceptions about:

1 standards of performance (individual and organisational) in a number of competency areas (patient care, management, teamwork, professional standards and consulting); and

2 the importance of these areas in terms of overall effectiveness and efficiency.

The output identifies areas of effective performance and areas in need of improvement. With suitable training you may be the person within your practice who could facilitate the use of this programme. More comprehensive details of the programme are available from the following sources:

• within Scotland: Scottish Council for Post Graduate Medical and Dental Education, 4th Floor, Hobart House, 80 Hanover Street, Edinburgh EH2 1EL

• outside Scotland: Edgecumbe Health, Edgecumbe Hall, Richmond Hill, Clifton, Bristol BS8 1AT.

Carrying out a communication audit

According to Rasberry and Lindsay (1994), an organisation's *communication climate* is the degree to which the system allows and encourages a free flow of ideas and information between employees. There are three components to a healthy climate: the quantity of information shared between employees, the quality of the content (which determines how well it accomplishes its purpose) and the number and nature of channels available for relaying information.

They suggest that you can test the climate in your organisation by asking the following questions. (We have amended some of the terminology to reflect the practice context rather than that of a commercial business organisation.)

Communication audit

1 Do you generally get enough information from the other people at work to do your job properly? (Include all members of the primary healthcare team, as relevant.)
2 Do you generally get more information than you need to do your job?
3 Does the information usually come when you need it, not when it's too late to be fully useful to you?
4 Is the information generally clear, relevant, accurate and consistent?
5 As a rule, do you know where to turn for information?
6 Can you get information from other people easily, without having to press them for it?
7 Do other people at work usually give you information directly and officially, or 'through the grapevine'?

The information gained from interviewing all practice team members using the questions listed above could identify some targets to improve the communication climate and generate an action plan. The same questions would then be used to re-audit the situation at an agreed later date. Full details of the tool appear at the end of this chapter.

Technique:	<div align="center">**Characterise your practice**</div>

Purpose: To provide an aid when determining the most appropriate type of development to instigate in the practice. Characterises the practice's current stability, ability to cope, change management culture and readiness to face the challenge of change.

Tips for use: Information on which to base the characterisation might be obtained from a knowledgeable but neutral Facilitator or practice development consultant brought in to conduct:

- systematic observation of practice day-to-day activities
- interviewing of all practice members
- and discussion based around a feedback report.

However, you may, as a practice, be able to make some reasoned judgements about **your own** general organisational state by using the diagnostic questions listed below as a starting point for discussion in facilitated groups.

Your role, depending on your position in the organisation and the influence you have as part of your remit, could be:

- to facilitate these groups
- to ascertain commonly held views
- and report back to the practice the general consensus of opinion about the topics covered in the questions – how it feels to work in the practice, what works well and what doesn't work so well, how people work together as a team, etc.

Whether an internal or external Facilitator, in addition to employing facilitation skills in these group meetings you need to pay attention to:

- how the whole concept is introduced to individuals in the practice
- to what extent anonymity of views is protected
- what the outcome of any discussions will be
- what the benefit to both the practice and individuals working in it is intended to be.

Done properly, this whole process is time consuming, **extremely demanding** of facilitative skill and not to be undertaken lightly.

Step by step process:

1 Following systematic data collection from observation/ interviews/feedback/discussion, select from the complete list of indicators (p. 73) the specific indicators which apply to the practice. You may want to add some further indicators from the information you have about the practice.

2 On the basis of the chosen indicators, assign a dimensional form for each of the four dimensions (pp. 74–5). Note that this involves some judgements on the part of the Facilitator and should be validated by the practice itself.

3 Highlight on the practice intervention sheet (p. 76) the columns which correspond to your chosen dimensional forms.

4 Enter a tick or cross in each highlighted cell, in line with those which appear on the master intervention sheet (p. 77). Check against the master intervention sheet for suggestions as to how best to intervene so as to progress the practice development. These are only suggestions and you may want to make additional or different ones of your own.

5 Agree with the practice any suggested proposed action or intervention.

Rerun or review the process after a specified period of time. The practice may exhibit different indicators at that point.

Materials required:

- Interview schedule diagnostic questions, *see* below.
- Complete list of dimensional forms and indicators (p. 73).
- Practice characterisation sheet (pp. 74–5).
- Practice intervention sheet (p. 76).
- Master intervention sheet (p. 77).

Alternative: You might use the list of dimensions and indicators as a focus for discussion in order to arrive at an agreed rapid appraisal.

Characterise your practice – diagnostic questions

1　What is it like to work here?
2　In your own words, could you say what this practice is about?
3　How well do people work together as a team in this practice?
4　Do you feel comfortable in your own role in the practice? Do other people understand your role?
5　How good is communication in this practice?
6　How are decisions taken? How are changes introduced? Are ideas taken on board?
7　How well does this practice keep up with workload and meet patient demand?
8　Systems. Is there room for improvement in these systems? What are the problem areas? What works really well? Why? Are things kept up to date? Who is responsible for keeping things up to date? What is done on the computer and what is done manually?
9　What role does the computer have in your own work?
10　Are you using it as efficiently as you might?
11　Do you see room for using it more?
12　How do you identify your continuing educational needs? What training have you had since joining the practice?
13　Do you feel your skills are fully utilised by the practice? Do your skills fully meet the needs of the job? Who identifies your training needs?
14　As a group of staff, what are your development needs?
15　As a practice, what are your development needs (clinical and organisational)? What are your reasons for citing these?
16　What encourages change in this practice? What inhibits it?
17　What do you understand by the term 'practice development plan' and how do you think it will benefit the practice?
18　What part do you hope to play in it?
19　Is there anything else you would like to add?

Characterising your practice – dimensions, forms and indicators

Dimension	Possible forms	Examples of indicators
1 *Organisational state*	Stable	i No major change in key personnel imminent or current (typically practice manager, often a partner) ii Partnership workable iii Management functional iv Systems adequate v Resources dependable vi Reasonable level of morale generally
	Unstable	*Any of the following indicators*: i Major change in key personnel current or imminent ii Moving to new premises iii Major alteration to practice systems, e.g. whole new computer system about to be installed iv Dysfunctional partnership v Widespread lack of confidence in management
2 *Current ability to cope*[a]	Coping	i 'Reasonable' waiting times for appointments ii Job satisfaction possible for most people iii No obvious problem with patient complaints iv Effective communication between different clinical and admin. groups
	Exhibiting acute problems	i A major incident occurring in the practice creating a 'shock' effect *Or a combination of two or more of:* ii Widespread low morale iii High staff turnover iv Poor performance in key areas v Obvious painful interpersonal problems, particularly within workgroups
	Exhibiting chronic problems	i General lack of job satisfaction ii Low morale iii Unsuitable premises affecting motivation iv Long-standing partnership problems v Lack of key resources vi Past failures to address problems
3 *Culture of change management*	Proactive	i Systems already in place for consultation, discussion, decision making and implementation of change ii Positive attitude to new ideas iii Practice able to review its own performance iv Practice accustomed to looking ahead

Characterising your practice – dimensions, forms and indicators (continued)

Dimension	Possible forms		Examples of indicators
	Reactive	i	Makes changes only in response to problems or directives
		ii	Nursing staff play no part in management decision making
		iii	Practice heavily focused on the day-to-day issues
4 *Development status*	Stuck	i	Lack of 'motivator' in the practice
		ii	No forum for all staff to express ideas
		iii	Widespread complacency
		iv	Relative isolation from proactive groups
		v	Becalmed after major organisational changes have bedded in
		vi	Tendency to be reactive rather than proactive
	Keen to develop but lacking skills	i	Ineffective implementation of good ideas
		ii	No established structure for planning systematically as a team
		iii	Anxiety about producing a plan for development
		iv	Can produce wealth of ideas and suggestions for development
		v	Would benefit from external support and training
		vi	Recognise the value of being proactive
	Poised for development	i	Have an established system of consultation, discussion, decision making, implementation and review of progress
		ii	Have experienced positive planned change
		iii	Possess appropriate skills and qualities in key people to manage and sustain change (motivation, leadership, commitment, enthusiasm, etc.)
		iv	Exhibit a cohesive partnership
		v	Have in place clear lines of communication within the team
		vi	Work within well-defined and understood roles
		vii	Show strong and effective management
		viii	Have a positive attitude to the challenge of change
		ix	Would benefit from an external viewpoint

[a] This second dimension suggests three forms – *coping*, *exhibiting acute problems* and *exhibiting chronic problems* – which are not necessarily mutually exclusive, since, for example, practices can exhibit both acute and chronic problems simultaneously. Additionally, they might possess some chronic problems but still be coping.

Practice characterisation sheet

- **Step 1**: for each dimension, fill in the specific diagnostic indicators which apply to your practice.
- **Step 2**: assign the most suitable dimensional form from the list of possible forms.

Dimension	Indicators found in this practice	Possible forms	Diagnosis of this practice[a]
Organisational state		Stable Unstable	
Current ability to cope		Coping Acute Chronic	
Culture of change management		Proactive Reactive	
Development status		Stuck Keen Poised	

[a] A 'positive' diagnosis can still accommodate some negative indicators.

Practice intervention sheet

- **Step 3**: highlight the columns on the practice intervention sheet which correspond to your chosen diagnosis.
- **Step 4**: checking against the master intervention sheet, enter a tick or cross in each of the highlighted cells.
- **Step 5**: look **across** the table for **each** intervention and find which ones have a tick present in **each** of the **highlighted** columns. Only where this condition applies will the intervention be recommended for the practice at this point in time.

Intervention	Dimension and form									
	1 *State*		2 *Coping ability*			3 *Culture*		4 *Development status*		
	Unstable	Stable	Coping	Acute	Chronic	Proactive	Reactive	Stuck	Keen	Poised
Interviews and feedback										
Development of process skills										
Initiate and support culture change (to that of proactive or team based culture)										
Provide impetus for major change in personnel or resources										
Facilitate structured organisational development										

Master intervention sheet

Intervention	Dimension and form									
	1 *Stability*		2 *Coping ability*			3 *Culture*		4 *Development status*		
	Unstable	Stable	Coping	Acute	Chronic	Proactive	Reactive	Stuck	Keen	Poised
Interviews and feedback	✔	✔	✔	✔	✔	✔	✔	✔	✔	✔
Development of process skills	×	✔	✔	×	✔	✔	✔	✔	✔	×
Initiate and support culture change (to that of proactive or team based culture)	×	✔	✔	×	✔	×	✔	✔	✔	×
Provide impetus for major change in personnel or resources	✔	✔	✔	✔	✔	×	✔	✔	✔	×
Facilitate structured organisational development	×	✔	✔	×	×	✔	×	×	×	✔

Key: ✔ = suitable

× = unsuitable/unnecessary

Technique:	**Team diagnostic summary**

Purpose: The following questionnaire evaluates areas of teamwork so that the collated results help the team to identify which areas are satisfactory and which are unsatisfactory. It is completed by each member of the team. Subjects choose a response from a number of options, which best fits their experience of knowledge of team goals, clarity of role, participation, decision making, managing conflict, availability of team members and mutual support.

The questionnaire is just one part of a comprehensive programme of team development piloted and refined in the Oxford area. It is reproduced with permission from Pritchard and Pritchard (1994) and is a modified version of a health team diagnostic instrument published in Plovnick *et al.* (1978).

Tips for use: Explain the benefits of using this tool to gain acceptance of it, e.g. it will act as a review of team effectiveness, diagnosing problems and identifying areas of good practice.

Each individual member of the team should complete the questionnaire anonymously. The results should be collated by the Facilitator and presented on a summary sheet. Copies of the summary are then issued to all team members and form the focus for a facilitated discussion on what should be the priority areas to address. Actual treatment would probably be the focus of discussion at a later date.

Some of the questions may appear quite threatening. It may feel more comfortable if questionnaires are completed on an anonymous basis and results collated by an external Facilitator.

Explain what will happen with the results, so that everyone is clear about what the next step will be.

Confidential questionnaire on teamworking: part 1

1 Team goals

Please read both statements, and ring one letter which seems closest to the way your team functions.

Statement 1: 'I often wonder why we work as a team. We seem to spend a lot of time and energy doing things which I do not think important, rather than concentrating on things which help us achieve our main goals.'

(a) Just like statement 1
(b) More like 1 than 2
(c) In between 1 and 2
(d) More like 2 than 1
(e) Just like statement 2

Statement 2: 'I am very clear about what our team is trying to achieve, and we put all our efforts into it. Whenever a question arises about what needs to be done we are able to get our priorities right by referring back to our main goals.'

Describe below any examples of situations in your team which illustrate your response to this question.

. . . .

. . . .

2 My job (role)

Please read both statements, and ring one letter which seems closest to the way your team functions.

Statement 1: 'Situations often arise in my job where I am uncertain what I am supposed to do. I am often not sure when something is my responsibility or someone else's. We never discuss what each of us thinks he or she, and other members of the team could or should do for best results.'

(a) Just like statement 1
(b) More like 1 than 2
(c) In between 1 and 2
(d) More like 2 than 1
(e) Just like statement 2

Statement 2: 'In almost every situation I am sure about what are my responsibilities, and what other team members are supposed to be doing. When a query arises, we discuss where we each think our responsibilities lie.'

Describe below any examples of situations in your team which illustrate your response to this question.

. . . .

. . . .

3   How things are done here: procedures

Participation
Please read both statements, and ring one letter which seems closest to the way your team functions.

Statement 1: 'When some people try to join in a discussion, they are often interrupted, or their suggestions ignored. People seem to pay attention to some team members, but not to others. Some people seem to do most of the talking, while others do not participate much or at all.'

(a)   Just like statement 1
(b)   More like 1 than 2
(c)   In between 1 and 2
(d)   More like 2 than 1
(e)   Just like statement 2

Statement 2: 'Everyone gets a chance to speak and to influence the discussion. We listen to everyone's contribution. No one is ignored. Everyone is drawn into the discussion.'

Examples:

. . . .

. . . .

Decisions
Please read both statements, and ring one letter which seems closest to the way your team functions.

Statement 1: 'After a discussion I often wonder what took place, and what is supposed to happen next. If I am expected to do something, I often do not agree with the task assigned to me. It seems that problems keep coming up for discussion when I thought we had decided about them.'

(a)   Just like statement 1
(b)   More like 1 than 2
(c)   In between 1 and 2
(d)   More like 2 than 1
(e)   Just like statement 2

Statement 2: 'When we discuss a problem, I usually understand exactly what the issue is, and what we have decided to do about it, and what are my responsibilities. Decisions make by the team are effectively carried out by team members.'

Examples:

. . . .

. . . .

Managing conflict

Please note that this is a different style of question.

First read all the statements, and then ring the one which most closely describes the situation in your team.

When a disagreement arises in the team:

(a) We assume it is best not to get too personal, so we let it pass and hope it will soon be forgotten. If feelings start to get heated, we try to cool things down by making the least of the disagreement (for example, 'there is no point in getting angry, so let's forget it').

(b) We often end the disagreement when someone takes charge and makes a decision, and it is not discussed further.

(c) We try to come to an agreement somewhere between the two conflicting positions. In other words we compromise, so everyone gains a little and loses a little and so we end the disagreement.

(d) We try to get the disagreeing parties together and let them talk through their points of view, until each can see some sense in the other's ideas. They we try to reach an agreement which makes sense to everyone.

Examples: . . . .

4 What it feels like to work in this team

Availability
Please read both statements, and ring one letter which seems closest to the way your team functions.

Statement 1: 'When you need to get hold of another team member, it is really difficult. Either they are not here, or they haven't got time to talk to you. But they seem to find time for other things.'

(a) Just like statement 1
(b) More like 1 than 2
(c) In between 1 and 2
(d) More like 2 than 1
(e) Just like statement 2

Statement 2: 'When you have a question, or need some help from another team member, there is no problem getting hold of anyone. People go out of their way to be available to each other. I have no difficulty talking to anyone on the team.'

Examples:

. . . .

. . . .

Mutual support
Please read both statements, and ring one letter which seems closest to the way your team functions.

Statement 1: 'This job is really frustrating. People do not seem to be concerned with helping others to get the job done. They go their own way. But if you try to do something different, or make a mistake, you get no help or support.'

(a) Just like statement 1
(b) More like 1 than 2
(c) In between 1 and 2
(d) More like 2 than 1
(e) Just like statement 2

Statement 2: 'I really like my job, and working in this team. The team encourages you to take responsibility. Other team members appreciate your efforts, and help when things are not going well. We really pull together in this team.'

Examples:

. . . .

. . . .

Team diagnostic summary sheet

Indicate on each bar the number of responses. The height of the bars or the scale used can be varied to suit the size of the practice.

1   Team goals

10

8

6

4

2

a   b   c   d   e

2   Clarity of role

10

8

6

4

2

a   b   c   d   e

3   Procedures
(a) participation

10

8

6

4

2

a   b   c   d   e

(b) decision making

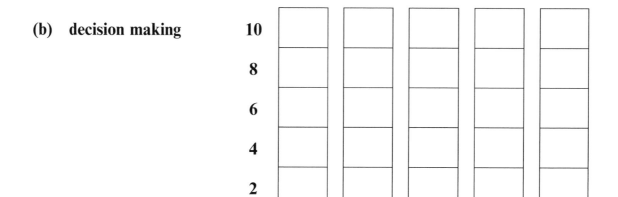

(c) managing conflict

4 Team relationships
(a) availability

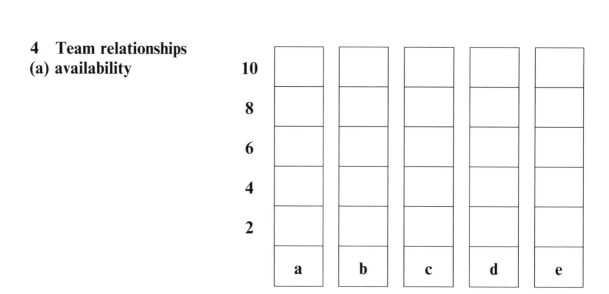

(b) mutual support

	a	b	c	d	e
10					
8					
6					
4					
2					

Technique:	**Communication audit**

Purpose: There are three components to a healthy climate of communication: the quantity of information shared between employees, the quality of the content (which determines how well it accomplishes its purpose) and the number and nature of channels available for relaying information.

You can test the climate in your organisation by asking the questions shown below, using the questions to form a questionnaire for self-completion by the members of your practice team.

Tips for use: Note that many of these questions are closed questions, i.e. you logically answer 'yes' or 'no'. To obtain more specific information you would also have to ask for details to explain the responses.

Alternatively, you might structure a one-to-one interview using the questions as a guide to the interviewer. Again, you would want to ask some open questions so that the interviewee would be encouraged to elaborate on their replies.

It is important that respondents know what will happen to the information gathered and whether individuals' identities will be kept secret or not.

Another alternative might be to structure a group discussion around the areas covered by the questionnaire.

You will need to record and collate responses so that patterns, common concerns and issues and individual differences can be identified. There are many books on questionnaire design and data recording and analysis which can guide you in this process. See, for example, Strauss and Corbin (1990).

Materials required: Communication audit questions.

Communication audit questions

1 Do you generally get enough information from the other people at work to do your job properly? (Include all members of the primary healthcare team, as relevant.)
2 Do you generally get more information than you need to do your job?
3 Does the information usually come when you need it, not when it's too late to be fully useful to you?
4 Is the information generally clear, relevant, accurate and consistent?
5 As a rule, do you know where to turn for information?
6 Can you get information from other people easily, without having to press them for it?
7 Do other people at work usually give you information directly and officially, or 'through the grapevine'?

Chapter 5

Instigating a programme of planned organisational change

Summary

In this chapter we outline briefly some organisational development processes used in the business world for the purpose of improving quality of service – namely BS 5750/ISO 9000, total quality management and benchmarking. We then contrast general practice with commercial business to indicate where it is essentially different in its current form.

There follows some general guidance to be considered before embarking on a programme of major change or development. We recommend that you think about your practice's current status, in terms of its:

- *organisational state*
- *current coping ability*
- *culture of change management*
- *readiness to face the challenge of change*

with a view to making some interim changes in climate or working procedures before undergoing significant reorganisation.

We describe some development tools for:

- *creating a vision for the future*
- *establishing a common understanding of strengths and weaknesses of the practice within its current context*

- *identifying training gaps*
- *structuring away-days*

and remind you of some basic facilitation techniques that you will need to draw on when engaging in practice development activities:

- *ice-breakers*
- *setting objectives*
- *brainstorming*
- *summarising*
- *giving feedback.*

Theory

Organisational development processes aimed at improving quality of service

Large-scale reorganisation in the wider business world is often undertaken in response to new ideology, as well as in the recognition that change is necessary in the organisation. Many organisations have embarked on a programme of organisational development in order to improve the quality of the service they provide. They may choose to subscribe to a whole new philosophy of organisational development. You may have heard of a number of well-known techniques for improving service quality (Pollitt, 1996), including the following.

- **BS 5750/ISO 9000**, which requires a system of accurately identifying customer requirements and the design and systematic use of documented procedures in the course of providing the best possible service to the customer.
- **Total quality management**, which requires setting of company goals based on improving quality, a commitment to quality throughout the organisation, a willingness to invest in training and an emphasis on avoiding mistakes before they occur.
- **Benchmarking**, which involves finding an organisation that is good at some particular process in which you also engage, studying the reasons for its good performance, making plans to raise your own performance to that level or beyond, implementing plans and then monitoring results.

There are examples to be found in the National Health Service of all these approaches. However, they do seem to pose some challenges, largely because they assume ways of running organisations that are not consistent with the way most of the NHS is traditionally run. Whatever the philosophy adopted, there is a need to manage the change process effectively so that systematic organisational development can be implemented and sustained.

The classic model of change management

The **classic model of change management** involves identifying the need to change, planning ways to make it happen, making the change and checking to see if the change has brought about the desired effect.

The three critical elements in effecting change are:

- *unfreezing*: creating the climate and conditions in the organisation such that the need for change is recognised and agreed; a diagnosis of the practice can provide this climate for change
- *changing*: providing all the support, training and monitoring necessary so that the change takes place; a recognition that change may bring a need for additional resources or training to meet new demands and that it is necessary to monitor implementation
- *refreezing*: ensuring that change has a lasting effect by gaining the commitment of members of the organisation to the new way of doing things; in effect, that the new way of doing things becomes part of the culture of the organisation after a period of time.

General Practice

Organisational development in general practice

In spite of some attempts to introduce business reorganisation principles into the health service, most practices still work largely within their own culture in effecting change – often a piecemeal approach. A comparison between business approaches to organisational development and characteristics of general practice might explain why this is so.

Business approaches	In general practice
• Place considerable emphasis on following chains of activity across organisations	• Work still tends to be compartmentalised along professional boundaries; district nurses organised independently of practice nurses, for example
• Demand a holistic, corporate approach, driven by management	• Practice management is still ill-defined and professions still tend to maintain their separate identities (and status)
• Require considerable investment of time and resources in quality-based training	• Time and resources are agreed to be in short supply in general practice
• Emphasise quality as based on the customer's perceptions	• There are large question marks over the patient's ability to shape primary care services
• Suggest the need for radical change	• This is rarely achievable in the day-to-day frenetic activity of many practices

In recent years, many practices have adopted a more systematic approach to organisational development, responding to the request from health boards for practice development plans. Tayside Health Board issued guidance for the production of practice development plans very much in line with that of Alison Wilson, in her 1994 publication *Changing Practices in Primary Care: A Facilitator's Handbook*, which suggests a number of steps to follow when embarking on any programme of change in general practice:

1 **It is important to plan or prepare for change by analysing the present situation, that is to ask:**
   • Why do we need to change?
   • What problems might we encounter along the way?
   • Who are the key people involved in the change?
   • Has such a change been done before?
   • What can we learn from our past experiences?

2   **A shared vision for the future allows the formation of goals or objectives that will enable the organisation to move to its desired state.**
   - Individuals who will be affected by the change ought to be given an opportunity to voice their opinions and concerns to help prevent obstruction or disruption later on.
   - Aims and objectives should always be written down so that achievements can be assessed later.
   - All possible methods of achieving change should be explored before a plan is devised.
   - Criteria for success should be defined at the planning stage.

3   **Armed with all the relevant information and having discussed all the possible choices, the practice should agree tasks and responsibilities.**
   - Most changes are best tackled as a team activity.
   - Realistic timetables should be set and stuck to as far as is possible.

4   **Every change should include a full evaluation or review.**
   - Have our aims been achieved? If not, why not?
   - Was the method used appropriate – best use of time, money and people?
   - What have been the costs and benefits of the change?
   - Have there been spin-off effects?
   - What lessons have been learnt?

5   **Any achievement requires acknowledgement and praise. This builds team cohesiveness, and provides motivation for further development.**

We will go on to describe how you might facilitate the process of organisational development.

Facilitate Your Own Practice

In thinking about a process of organisational development, your role again will depend on your position and responsibilities within the practice. It may be that you can influence the process by suggesting techniques or posing questions about the process. If management of the practice is part of your remit, you may be able to design and guide the whole process from a leading position. There are many guides to change management available from libraries and booksellers and we will include details of some useful techniques in the Tips and Tools section which follows this section. However, for now we want to concentrate on thinking about how the process might run in your own individual practice.

Some important questions when thinking about large-scale development of the practice

1 Are we **stable** enough at present to undergo major organisational change?
2 Can we **cope** with the impact and ramifications of such change and still fulfil our day-to-day responsibilities?
3 Do we **demonstrate positive attitudes** to change?
4 Do we have in place the **processes** needed to manage significant change?

(You might want to refer back to the Practice Characterisation Model described on pp. 70–7.)

Reviewing and evaluating the FED project (Duffy *et al.*, 1998), the Facilitators involved agreed that to manage significant change a practice needs to possess the following:

Practice resources needed to manage significant change

- Partners who can communicate their vision for the future of the practice.
- Appropriate leadership.
- Effective decision making based on adequate information and consultation.
- Clear lines of communication within the team.
- Clarity and understanding of roles.
- A 'motivator' within the team.
- Enthusiasm and commitment of all concerned.
- Regular review of progress and flexibility in approach.

If it does not, it may be that there are one or more areas to concentrate on first. We have described how most practices tend to concentrate on tasks and action rather than the process of working to achieve the end result. Similarly, when it comes to planning for the future in a systematic, large-scale fashion, the focus tends to be on 'the practice development plan' or 'our priorities for the next five years', rather than on how **the existing structure and culture** of the organisation will have a bearing on the successful creation and implementation of any master plan.

We suggest that a **characterisation** of your practice – a diagnosis of the organisational state – can help guide the practice towards problem areas of the practice culture and organisation. These might need to be addressed first to prepare the practice to embark on a programme of organisational change, so to improve the chances of successful management of the situation. We have already shown a questioning route which helped recently in diagnosing practices in Tayside (*see* Case Study 5). Using that type of diagnostic process we could characterise the organisation of a practice along four dimensions of:

- organisational state (stability)
- current coping ability
- change management culture
- readiness to face the challenge of change.

If a practice is **unstable** (and the reasons for this may be many and varied), it is unlikely that a full-scale programme of organisational change will work. Similarly, if a practice is **not coping** on a day-to-day basis, the effort involved in major change will not be sustainable. If the culture is commonly a **reactive** one, then the processes involved in planning, implementing and reviewing a programme of change will be alien to many people and thus not 'bought into' nor considered important or necessary. If the practice is not adequately **prepared** to face the challenge of change, in that it lacks the procedures, systems, skills and personal qualities which are required for managing a major change process, then it is unlikely to succeed without some prior development work.

Sometimes a practice needs to settle down after a major upheaval, e.g. a move to new premises. Occasionally dramatic action is required to solve an acute or chronic problem, e.g. the resignation of a partner or replacement of the practice manager, both of which would then seriously affect the stability of the practice for a period of time.

Interim alternatives to full-scale development, which would help to create a suitable climate and culture to support future major change, might include the following:

- broadening of the decision-making group to take account of all team members' views
- team building
- development of the practice manager role to focus more on 'management' tasks
- resolution of partnership difficulties.

However, in the event that conditions **are suitable** for embarking on a programme of planned organisational change, there are a number of well-practised tools and techniques to guide and structure the process.

Tools and Tips

We will outline briefly here some tools to aid the process of organisational development, which are all described fully at the end of the chapter. As always it is important that:

- **you** understand how to use the tool
- **you** feel comfortable with the tool yourself
- you can **explain** to others the **benefits** of using a specific tool
- you can **allay any fears** about participating
- you can **give explicit instructions** to others
- they **know** what the **outcome** is likely to be

and, above all, that you have **the agreement of the group** to use this tool before you go ahead.

To create a vision for the future in order to stimulate ideas and plans for change you might suggest using '**best practice**'. This tool encourages synergy within a practice by stimulating creativity and inspiration, and creating shared goals. It asks each individual on his or her own, and then as a member of the whole group, to think about what it would be like to be a patient in the **ideal** practice and how it would feel to work there.

To reach a shared understanding of the strengths and weaknesses of the practice in the context of both the current situation and the predictable future, you can facilitate a '**SWOT analysis**'. This technique encourages identification of the strengths and weaknesses of the practice in the context of existing and predicted opportunities and threats, and thus encourages development of a comprehensive picture, warts and all, of the practice by its members.

To identify training gaps once the practice has established its goals, there are a number of training needs analysis tools in existence. We would refer you to the Gower publication *Training Needs Analysis* (Bartram and Gibson, 1994) and also to a more recent Welsh Office handbook entitled *The 'IT' Files* (1997) from which we include one of their tools, a computer training needs analysis, which proved useful to a Tayside practice who were beginning to develop an information management strategy. This training needs analysis, entitled 'Computer tasks and skills analysis', investigated individuals' current level of knowledge and skills in a range of computer-based tasks, in relation to the importance of these tasks to their job role.

We have already described action plans and responsibility charts in Chapter 3. These take some time to discuss and devise. Many practices now participate in 'away-days' in order to produce such plans. We conclude this section with some advice on planning, running, evaluating and feeding back to the practice, on away-days and other practice 'events'.

Providing structure has already been identified as a key Facilitator skill. This is particularly important when planning and running away-days so that the time and money spent on such an activity is seen to be worthwhile.

If you are facilitating an away-day in your own practice there are some basic useful steps to follow.

1 Establish the objectives for the day.
2 Agree who should participate in the day. (Is it a day for partners, or for the whole team, for example?)
3 Design a format that will allow you to meet your objectives, maintain momentum and generate positive feelings within participants.
4 Agree the format with the decision-making group in the practice.
5 Select a venue and a time that will be convenient for all those participating and conducive to the type of activity you intend to incorporate.
6 Establish how the event will be evaluated.
7 Organise any equipment or materials in advance.
8 Visit the venue before the event and check its suitability for your purpose.
9 Be flexible on the day if plans prove to be inappropriate in some way.
10 Review proceedings soon after the event so that lessons can be learnt for any future session.

We have included a workshop pro forma in the Tools section at the end of the chapter, to help the Facilitator in planning and reviewing such events.

Case study 8 shows the programme for an away-day run by the Olive Practice, who were under pressure to meet a deadline for producing a practice development plan. This is a detailed programme, which demonstrates a very directive approach by the Facilitator in terms of structuring the day (as agreed with the partners and practice manager). Note how the Facilitator has attempted to keep the momentum of the day going by varying the activities and the groupings, and how the whole day is geared towards achieving the objective. Within that programme you will see evidence of many of the tools and techniques described in this handbook and in Duffy and Griffin (1999) – setting objectives and ground rules, clarifying the role of the Facilitator, brainstorming, visioning, small groupwork, setting priorities, action planning and evaluating.

The Facilitator's preparation checklist for this event details a wide range of issues and arrangements which had to be taken into account in the pre-planning. The seemingly relaxed but productive tone of the day and the positive, enthusiastic approach of the Facilitator were possible only as a result of considerable advance deliberation by the Facilitator, and her clarification of the requirements, attitudes, expectations and hopes of the practice.

The Facilitator played a key role in both the planning and the running of the day. Feedback from the practice was very positive, expressing a sense of achievement, satisfaction and regeneration of interest in the future of the practice.

Case Study 8
The Olive Practice away-day:
detailed programme and Facilitator's checklist

09.00	**Welcome**	Coffee on arrival Welcome and introductions	*GP*
09.05	**What we will do today**	Outline plan for the day Explanation of the Facilitator role Establishing objectives and ground rules	*Facilitator*
09.20	**Thinking about the future of the practice**	GPs to share with each other their vision of the future and the values that underpin it. To devise plan for the development of the organisation and clinical services over next 5 years. Prepare short presentation of these to be given to the whole group	
		Nursing team to prepare a 10-minute presentation of their plans and priorities for the development of their service, including justification for their ideas	*Small groups*
		Admin. staff to discuss and agree their list of priorities for development of their area of work (may be done in advance of the meeting and a representative sent) and prepare short presentation	
10.30		Coffee	
10.45	**The GPs' vision**	Doctors present their vision for the practice	*GP*

Time	Topic	Details	Who
10.50	**Our groups' priorities**	Each group presents their priorities for the development of the practice and answers questions from the rest of the team	*GP/Nursing/ Admin.*
11.45	**Our reactions**	Small group discussion of ideas raised, impact on individuals, training gaps, staffing requirements, individual concerns, etc.	*Small multi-disciplinary groups*
12.30		LUNCH	
14.00	**Sharing views**	Feedback from small groups	*Reps from each group*
14.15	**Deciding priorities** **Identifying resources needed**	Review of all priorities Agreement on list of priorities Establishment of approximate order of priorities, e.g. 1 yr, 2 yr, 5 yr Brief review of any staffing, training or resource requirements associated with these priorities	*Facilitator to facilitate open discussion and subsequent decision making*
15.00	**What should be in the plan?**	Requirements of practice development plan	*Practice manager*
15.15		Coffee	
15.30	**This is how we will complete the plan on time**	Establishment of existing information and what needs to be collected Agreement on who will obtain and/or provide any information not currently available Action plan for writing the development plan Arrangements for reviewing the draft plan Arrangements for beginning the development of the practice	*Facilitated discussion and decision making*
16.45	**How did the day go?**	Conclusion and evaluation	*Facilitator and whole group*
17.00		Close	*GP*

Facilitator's checklist

Relationship with practice	Establish key objectives of management team
	Discuss practice past experiences of similar events
	Clarify away-day roles and expectations
	Determine who will be attending
	Prepare draft format for the day for further discussion
	Agree final programme
	Establish how practice staff are to be informed about the day
	Establish the nature and timing of any report to be produced
	Agree on how you will get feedback on the Facilitator role
	Agree invoicing and payment procedure
Programme	Allocation of time
	Introductions
	Slot for pharmaceutical representative . . .
	Ice-breaker
	Ground rules
	Presenting or setting of objectives
	Housekeeping issues
	Reference to Facilitator (and other) roles
	Recording of information – how and by whom
	Information-sharing slots
	Discussion
	Decision making
	Group activities – composition of groups, design of activities and instructions, feeding back
	Summaries – when and by whom
	Revisit objectives
	Closing remarks
	Evaluation – format, collation of responses, how to feed back to practice
Interaction issues	Stimulating commitment to, and enthusiasm for, the day
	Creating and sustaining the appropriate tone for the whole day
	Encouraging participation

	Establish whether all share the same knowledge of events in the practice
	Participants' needs from the day (as opposed to the management group)
	Size of small groups for group activities
	Generation of ideas – stimulus and techniques
	Potential status or interpersonal problems – what are they, how to deal with
	Dealing with tension
	Keeping momentum going
	Celebrating achievements
	Effective closing to the day
Environment	Liaise with hotel management
	Contact rep and clarify involvement/resources
	Check out suitability of accommodation and facilities
	Finalise details of booking
	Arrange timing and location of refreshments and lunch
	Detail initial layout of main meeting room and breakout room
	Locate toilets
	Organise provision and positioning of overhead projector, flip charts, other visual aids
	Pens, Blue tack, paper, Post-its, etc.
	Check lighting, temperature and ventilation
	Organise seating arrangements
	Name tags
	Ensure adequate working space

When planning to facilitate an away-day or similar significant activity in a practice, you will be able to draw ideas and tools from a plethora of management resource handbooks available in your local college or university library. When selecting tools, and possibly amending them for specific use in general practice, we can only reiterate our earlier advice to consider in advance the following questions:

- What is the purpose of using this tool?
- What will be the potential cost in terms of time, effort and resources?
- Will this activity make good use of the practice's time, effort and resources?
- Can every person in the practice see its relevance and thus be committed to it?

- What are people's concerns about this activity? (Better to get these out into the open and address them.)
- What procedures will have to be in place to carry out the activity?
- What will we do with the results?

We now conclude this section with full details of tools described earlier:

- best practice
- SWOT analysis
- training needs analysis (computer tasks and skills)
- workshop pro forma.

These will both complement and require the use of more basic facilitation techniques such as:

- ice-breakers
- setting objectives
- brainstorming
- summarising
- giving feedback,

the majority of which were first described in volume 1 but are also reproduced here for completeness.

Despite all the advance planning and structuring, the Facilitator's skill on the day remains to be fully attentive to all aspects of the interaction, to intervene for the benefit of the group, to be flexible in modifying plans and procedures where necessary, and to create and sustain a positive, honest and productive atmosphere. You may want to consult or revisit volume 1 in this series (Duffy and Griffin, 1999) to remind yourself of these important aspects of working with groups.

Technique: **Best practice**

Purpose: To help the practice create a vision for the future.

Tips for use:
- Creating a vision for the future is useful in encouraging synergy within a group – by stimulating creativity and inspiration and creating shared goals.
- It can also be used at the start of a development programme to produce ideas for 'where we want to be'.
- Encourage participants to think as broadly as possible within the bounds of reality.
- There are no right or wrong answers – only pointers for discussion.
- Members of the group work as individuals first and then come together as a whole group, or as a subgroup and then a whole group.
- The skill of the person facilitating is in:
  - bringing together all the disparate ideas from individuals
  - grouping together ones which broadly mean the same
  - focusing the whole group on the range of ideas from which to pick the three main ones
  - encouraging discussion
  - suggesting a technique for reaching consensus if this is proving difficult (e.g. nominal group technique – *see* Chapter 3)
- Commitment to participate in further activities of this nature will be greater if some **action** is then taken on the basis of the 'best practice' scenario.

Materials required:
- Best practice 1 questions for each group member, *see* below.
- Best practice 2 questions, one sheet per group, *see* below.
- Flip chart to collate individual responses.
- Record of group's final choices.

Best practice 1

Imagine yourself as a **patient** attending the best general practice surgery ever. Write down three things that strike you about what it would be like to be dealt with as a patient in this ideal practice.

1

2

3

Imagine yourself **working** in the best general practice surgery ever. Write down three things that strike you about what it would be like to work in this ideal practice.

1

2

3

Best practice 2

Compare the points you have written individually, and **as a group** pick the top three things that you feel would strike **a patient** about the way they are dealt with in this ideal practice.

1

2

3

Compare the points you have written individually, and **as a group** pick the top three things that would strike **an employee** about what it is like to work in this ideal practice.

1

2

3

Technique: **SWOT analysis**

Purpose: 'SWOT' analysis is a tool used in management to highlight the areas where changes could be made. It does this by helping identify:

- **Strengths**, i.e. what does the practice do well?
- **Weaknesses**, i.e. what is not working so well? Are there areas where the practice's resources and skills could be developed more?
- **Opportunities**, i.e. are there things happening now which the practice will be able to take advantage of and benefit from (e.g. outside changes)?
- **Threats**, i.e. what changes do you see as potentially disadvantageous, e.g. policy changes, new services being provided by other practices in competition?

Tips for use: The SWOT analysis can cover any aspect of how the practice works as an organisation or how it delivers its clinical service to patients. (If you feel there's too much to go on one SWOT diagram, you can do 'organisational' and 'clinical' diagrams.)

Once the SWOT analysis is plotted out, it is much easier to see what areas practice goals should target, e.g. if 'use of information technology' was identified as a weakness, then a goal could be 'to improve the use of information technology in the practice'.

Use the headings to list the main factors that apply to your practice. You can either brainstorm (see later in this section) with the whole practice team, or ask each group within the practice to construct their own list, which would be collated on to a master sheet. An example of a SWOT analysis is shown below.

Example of a practice SWOT analysis

Strengths	Weaknesses
• Happy practice with effective working relationships • Good working relationship between GPs • Developed sense of teamwork • Sense of motivation and willingness to innovate • Close identification of community nurses and community pharmacist with practice	• A lot of staff turnover recently • Administrative structure lacks clarity and definition of roles • Formal communication structures underdeveloped • Not all innovations shared or carried through by the whole practice
Opportunities	Threats
• New GP promising period of stability • Staff looking for new roles • Time for practice manager to concentrate less on locum management and more on internal administration development • Stimulation of practice development and learning as a result of involvement in a university project	• More staff changes • Staff budget restrictions from primary care trust • Time constraints to maintaining new structured meetings

Technique:	**Computer tasks and skills analysis**

Purpose: To identify skills gaps in relation to computer and other information management skills. Helps when generating a training plan for the practice team.

This training needs analysis is adapted from the one produced by the Welsh Office (1997).

Tips for use: Can be used for individual appraisal or training needs analysis.

Results can also be collated to see where significant competence gaps exist in key areas.

Materials required:
- One copy of staff profile per person (*see* below). You may want to add some practice-specific items to the questionnaire or delete some irrelevant items.
- Collation sheet.

Some questions you might want to ask when the results are collated

1 Practice profile
- Can all essential tasks be covered at all times of the day/week, especially in situations of illness/holidays?
- Are some features of the computer system being underused?
- Are the skills held in the right people?
- Are the people with the skills able to pass them on to colleagues, i.e. do they have the time, are they in close contact?
- Is the level and spread of skills available suitable for the overall needs of the practice (e.g. for audit, patient summaries, health promotion)?

2 Collated staff group profile
- Are individuals generally aware of the possible role of some of the computer facilities in their own work?
- Do any individuals lack key skills which they have identified as important for their position?
- Are any skills being underused which might benefit the practice?
- Is there disparity amongst skills in a particular group of staff, e.g. GPs?
- Are there any specific areas mentioned by individuals where they express a particular need for training?
- What might the next steps be in using the information in relation to meeting training needs?

Staff profile: computer tasks and skills analysis

Name . . . . Position . . . .

Hours worked/week: . . . .

Date completed . . . .

Below you are asked to consider your job role and the level of knowledge/skills you currently possess. Alongside each of the tasks is a scale of 0 to 4: please circle the number which most applies to you.

Importance to job role
0 = No importance
1 = Low
2 = Would be useful
3 = It is important that I have a sound understanding of this
4 = It is essential to my job role

Current level of knowledge/skills
0 = No knowledge
1 = Some awareness
2 = Basic understanding
3 = Intermediate level
4 = Advanced level

	Importance to job role					Current level of knowledge/skills				
Access the system	0	1	2	3	4	0	1	2	3	4
Registration										
Add new patients	0	1	2	3	4	0	1	2	3	4
Patient transfers	0	1	2	3	4	0	1	2	3	4
CHS registrations	0	1	2	3	4	0	1	2	3	4
Change of reg. details	0	1	2	3	4	0	1	2	3	4
Medical history										
View history screen	0	1	2	3	4	0	1	2	3	4
Add clinical data	0	1	2	3	4	0	1	2	3	4
Add admin. data (e.g. new patients)	0	1	2	3	4	0	1	2	3	4
Run history searches	0	1	2	3	4	0	1	2	3	4

	Importance to job role					Current level of knowledge/skills				
Therapy										
View therapy screen (repeat prescriptions)	0	1	2	3	4	0	1	2	3	4
Issue repeat prescriptions	0	1	2	3	4	0	1	2	3	4
Modify prescribing info.	0	1	2	3	4	0	1	2	3	4
Add acute prescriptions	0	1	2	3	4	0	1	2	3	4
Add repeat prescriptions	0	1	2	3	4	0	1	2	3	4
Maintain drug formulary	0	1	2	3	4	0	1	2	3	4
Run therapy searches	0	1	2	3	4	0	1	2	3	4
Prevention										
View prevention screen	0	1	2	3	4	0	1	2	3	4
Find test results	0	1	2	3	4	0	1	2	3	4
Add smear results	0	1	2	3	4	0	1	2	3	4
Add contraception	0	1	2	3	4	0	1	2	3	4
Add immunisations	0	1	2	3	4	0	1	2	3	4
Add test results	0	1	2	3	4	0	1	2	3	4
Add recalls	0	1	2	3	4	0	1	2	3	4
Run prevention searches	0	1	2	3	4	0	1	2	3	4
Appointments*										
Prepare appointment sheets	0	1	2	3	4	0	1	2	3	4
Take advance bookings	0	1	2	3	4	0	1	2	3	4
Check arrivals in	0	1	2	3	4	0	1	2	3	4
* See separate sheet for more detailed listing										
Clinical management screens										
Add health promotion data	0	1	2	3	4	0	1	2	3	4
Add new patient medical data	0	1	2	3	4	0	1	2	3	4
Other freehand screens (specify)										
....	0	1	2	3	4	0	1	2	3	4
....	0	1	2	3	4	0	1	2	3	4
Searches and reports										
Miscellaneous searches	0	1	2	3	4	0	1	2	3	4
Run capitation report	0	1	2	3	4	0	1	2	3	4
Run target reports	0	1	2	3	4	0	1	2	3	4

	Importance to job role					Current level of knowledge/skills				
Run referral report	0	1	2	3	4	0	1	2	3	4
Run health promotions report	0	1	2	3	4	0	1	2	3	4
Run other searches (specify)										
. . . .	0	1	2	3	4	0	1	2	3	4
. . . .	0	1	2	3	4	0	1	2	3	4
. . . .	0	1	2	3	4	0	1	2	3	4

Coding

Read codes	0	1	2	3	4	0	1	2	3	4

Other skills

Backup	0	1	2	3	4	0	1	2	3	4
Keyboard skills	0	1	2	3	4	0	1	2	3	4
Computer terminology	0	1	2	3	4	0	1	2	3	4
Medical terminology	0	1	2	3	4	0	1	2	3	4
Word processing	0	1	2	3	4	0	1	2	3	4
Use of spreadsheets	0	1	2	3	4	0	1	2	3	4
Use of databases	0	1	2	3	4	0	1	2	3	4
Use of graphics	0	1	2	3	4	0	1	2	3	4
Windows	0	1	2	3	4	0	1	2	3	4
Negotiation skills	0	1	2	3	4	0	1	2	3	4
Presentation skills	0	1	2	3	4	0	1	2	3	4
Communication skills	0	1	2	3	4	0	1	2	3	4
Accounts	0	1	2	3	4	0	1	2	3	4
Payroll	0	1	2	3	4	0	1	2	3	4
Desktop publishing	0	1	2	3	4	0	1	2	3	4
Use of telephone system	0	1	2	3	4	0	1	2	3	4

Troubleshooting
Printers:

Change ribbons/cartridges	0	1	2	3	4	0	1	2	3	4
Loading paper	0	1	2	3	4	0	1	2	3	4

Procedures to follow when:

Medical system fails	0	1	2	3	4	0	1	2	3	4
Network fails	0	1	2	3	4	0	1	2	3	4
Power failures/surges	0	1	2	3	4	0	1	2	3	4
How to reboot system	0	1	2	3	4	0	1	2	3	4

	Importance to job role					Current level of knowledge/skills				
Reboot link to branch site	0	1	2	3	4	0	1	2	3	4
Signing off whole system	0	1	2	3	4	0	1	2	3	4
Anti-virus checking, when/how	0	1	2	3	4	0	1	2	3	4

Accessing external help

Contacting software supplier	0	1	2	3	4	0	1	2	3	4
Contacting hardware supplier	0	1	2	3	4	0	1	2	3	4

Dispensing

Re-ordering system	0	1	2	3	4	0	1	2	3	4
Producing labels	0	1	2	3	4	0	1	2	3	4
Running system upgrades	0	1	2	3	4	0	1	2	3	4
Running backups	0	1	2	3	4	0	1	2	3	4
Other specified tasks	0	1	2	3	4	0	1	2	3	4

. . . .

. . . .

Further comments

. . . .

. . . .

. . . .

. . . .

. . . .

APPOINTMENT SYSTEM

	Importance to job role					Current level of knowledge/skills				
Signing on	0	1	2	3	4	0	1	2	3	4
Refreshing screen	0	1	2	3	4	0	1	2	3	4
Types of books	0	1	2	3	4	0	1	2	3	4
Types of slots	0	1	2	3	4	0	1	2	3	4
To make a booking	0	1	2	3	4	0	1	2	3	4
To cancel a booking	0	1	2	3	4	0	1	2	3	4
To make a special booking	0	1	2	3	4	0	1	2	3	4
Reviewing an appointment	0	1	2	3	4	0	1	2	3	4
When a patient arrives	0	1	2	3	4	0	1	2	3	4
Inserting a slot	0	1	2	3	4	0	1	2	3	4
Making a slot available	0	1	2	3	4	0	1	2	3	4
Removing a slot	0	1	2	3	4	0	1	2	3	4
Moving an appointment	0	1	2	3	4	0	1	2	3	4
Copying an appointment	0	1	2	3	4	0	1	2	3	4
Printing appointment list	0	1	2	3	4	0	1	2	3	4
Searches	0	1	2	3	4	0	1	2	3	4
Find patient's appointment	0	1	2	3	4	0	1	2	3	4
Inserting a session	0	1	2	3	4	0	1	2	3	4
End of day close down	0	1	2	3	4	0	1	2	3	4

Thank you for completing this computer tasks and skills analysis. The information will be collated and matched against the needs of the practice.

Technique:	<div align="center">**Away-day planning**</div>

Purpose: Away-days present a unique opportunity in an otherwise very busy working schedule to take time out to discuss important issues, plan for the future, review progress after major change and build the team. Providing a structure is always one of the key Facilitator skills. Away-days, above all, need to have a carefully planned structure, geared to the agreed objectives for the day but flexible enough to respond to events on the day. We enclose some pro formas to aid your planning and review processes.

Tips: *If you are facilitating an away-day in your own practice there are some basic useful steps to follow:*

1 Establish the objectives for the day.
2 Agree who should participate in the day. (Is it a day for partners, or for the whole team, for example?)
3 Design a format that will allow you to meet your objectives, maintain momentum and generate positive feelings within participants.
4 Agree the format with the decision-making group in the practice.
5 Select a venue and a time that will be convenient for all participating and conducive to the type of activity you intend to incorporate.
6 Establish how the event will be evaluated.
7 Organise any equipment or materials in advance.
8 Visit the venue before the event and check its suitability for your purpose.
9 Be flexible on the day if plans prove to be inappropriate in some way.
10 Review proceedings soon after the event so that lessons can be learnt for any future session.

You may also want to consult the Facilitator's checklist in Case Study 8.

OUTLINE DETAILS OF FACILITATED ACTIVITY	
Event	
Date/time	
Venue	
Contact person	
Purpose of meeting	
Objectives • • • •	
Draft programme • • • • • • • •	
Who is to be there?	
Equipment to be made available	
Equipment/materials to bring	
Evaluation arrangements	
Other	

Post Workshop Evaluation by Manager/Partner/Management Team	
Context	
	To what extent did the day address issues relevant to the needs of the practice?
Input	
	What did you think of the way the day was structured?
	What was your opinion of the content of the programme?
	Should we have done anything differently with hindsight?
	Do you think the right people were there?
	Do you have any comments on the Facilitator's role?

Reactions	
	What did you think of the day at the time?
	What do you think of the day now?
	Did you get out of it what you were hoping to get out of it?
	Would you repeat this type of away-day?

Outcomes
Which of the objectives for the day were met?
Which of the objectives for the day were not met?
What is going to happen in the practice as a result of the day?
Do you have any other comments?

Signed:	**Date:**

Technique:	**Ice-breakers**

Purpose: To help create a suitable environment to achieve the goals of the meeting. Depending on the group, the purpose of the meeting, how well group members know each other already and your familiarity with the group, the prime need might be:

- to find out each other's names
- to get to know one another better
- to focus minds on the business of the day
- to express any hopes and fears about what might happen that day
- to become mentally alert.

Tips for use:
- Be clear about what is the primary need of the group at the start of the meeting or activity.
- Select an ice-breaker which best meets the needs of the group.
- Keep it simple and short, particularly if the group is large.
- Be sensitive to how the ice-breaker might affect participants.

Materials required:
- Simple instructions given verbally or written on a flip chart or overhead.
- Alternative: a set of cards for ice-breakers where the activity involves participants answering a question.

There are many examples of ice-breakers in training manuals. The following are a selection which have proved acceptable in primary care settings locally.

Adjectival Annie

A light-hearted ice-breaker which allows participants to learn each other's names. Each member of the group in turn states their Christian name, prefixed by an adjective beginning with the same letter as their name, and which best describes them. For example, 'Hi, I am zany Zelda'. A useful variation when you are working with an established group as an outsider, is to ask each member to describe the person on their right using one word only. This usually generates some hilarity in the group.

What have you left behind?

Suggest to the group that they each think of a mental obstacle linked to home or work, which might interfere with their full participation in the group – is the ironing left undone, or does the grass need cutting, or do those patient notes need to be updated? Whatever it might be, suggest that they give themselves permission to set it aside for today. Share your own thoughts with the group, and ask if anyone else would like to do the same.

Get up and move around

Physical activity centred round a requirement to mingle with others can help overcome initial reticence to participate in the group, a feeling of sluggishness at the start of the day or after a heavy meal. You can suggest that the group form a line in order of height, or shoe size, or birthday. To make it harder you can outlaw speaking.

Express hopes, wishes and concerns

It may aid participation if all members are given an opportunity to express their feelings about taking part. You can prepare in advance a number of cards, each with one question on it, and ask each member to select one from the pack. Questions might include:

- What do I most dread about today?
- What do I hope we will achieve today?
- What will help us get the job done today?

The members of the group, in turn, read out their question and give their answer.

Technique:	**Setting objectives for a group activity or meeting**

Purpose:
- To give structure to work of the group.
- To provide a focus for discussion or other activity.
- To stimulate review of achievement.

For a single meeting, its **objectives** (or **goals**) are its terms of reference. For *any* meeting a clear statement of its objectives will encourage all discussion and energy to be directed towards achieving these.

Tips for use: Clarify whether it is appropriate for you to set the objectives in advance, following discussion with the group or not, or whether the objectives will be decided at the meeting by the group with your help.

Ensure that objectives are **SMART** (*see* below).

It may be useful to display the objectives throughout the meeting, e.g. on a large poster.

Materials required:
- Flip chart or overhead projector.
- Printed statement if objectives are set in advance of the meeting.

'**SMART**' objectives are:

Specific — The wording should leave no doubt about what is required.

Measurable — The goal or objective should be readily measurable, and the results should be available quickly and regularly.

Attainable — If the goal offers poor chances of success, then it becomes a demotivating force.

Relevant — Goals must be seen to be relevant to the goals of both the organisation and the individual.

Timebound — How much and how soon must be spelt out – otherwise the goal is little more than a 'wish'.

Objectives should be written in terms of action and so usually begin with a verb. For example, in a meeting to discuss whether or not to adopt a new guideline for disease management, the objectives might be:

- To **achieve** a common understanding of the content of the guideline.
- To **agree** our criteria for evaluating this guideline.
- To **establish** the impact on individuals of any change in practice.
- To **identify** any new resources which might be required if the guideline is adopted.
- To **discuss** the costs and benefits of adopting the guideline.
- To **reach** consensus amongst the group on whether or not to adopt it.

Technique:	**Brainstorming**

Purpose:
- To generate a wide variety of ideas in a short space of time.
- To produce novel or creative ideas.

Tips for use:
- Write the problem or topic where all members of the group can see it – on a flip chart for example.
- Encourage expression of all ideas, however zany.
- Make sure that everyone understands that no judgements should be made about the quality of ideas.
- Agree how the ideas will be elicited – in a round, by shouting out or by writing on Post-its.

Materials required:
- Flip chart.
- Post-its (optional).

General rules of brainstorming

1 Clearly state the purpose of the activity.
2 Each person takes a turn, expressing one idea at a time.
3 No one to criticise or comment.
4 Every idea is accepted as a good one.
5 It is all right to pass if you have nothing to say.
6 Record all ideas verbatim, in a visible place to stimulate new ideas in the group. Do not paraphrase or reword.
7 Seek clarification of an idea where it would help the group.
8 Group together similar concepts if appropriate.

Variations

Free-form brainstorming: anyone can offer an idea as soon as it comes to mind. This produces a relaxed atmosphere and encourages creativity, although not all may contribute. It may be difficult to write quickly enough to keep up with the flow of ideas. Consider enlisting a scribe (or even two) to help out.

Structured brainstorming: ideas are solicited in a round, each member speaking in turn. This is more rigid in format and may inhibit spontaneity.

Silent brainstorming: ideas are written on Post-its – one idea per Post-it – and then displayed for all to see. All have an equal 'voice', some more reticent members might feel more confident about contributing, but group synergy is lost. The Post-its can be grouped in a variety of ways and the volume and spread can be graphic illustrations of the nature or scope of a problem.

The product of brainstorming is a list of ideas which can then be discussed.

Technique:	**Summarising**

Purpose:
- To paraphrase a rambling or long and detailed contribution by one speaker in the group.
- To pull together a number of threads from a discussion.
- To increase the clarity of meetings.
- To deal with negative feelings in a group.
- To indicate the current state of progress so that the group can see a way forward.

Tips for use:
- This is a key facilitation skill which can really help the group move on.
- It requires active listening by the Facilitator. It is a demanding activity!
- Keeping notes of discussion, either for personal use or on a flip chart visible to the whole group, helps the task of summarising.
- Try to find common features within the content of discussion or the output from group activity. Grouping according to common features, e.g. clinical service, management of information, development of teamwork, can help bring together a wide range of ideas into some coherent structure.
- If small groups are working on tasks, encourage them to structure any feedback to the whole group so that disparate ideas are already grouped.
- Underline, label or highlight in some way, key words and issues. You can use different colours or numbering systems to show links between various ideas and concepts.
- You should avoid making any direct judgements about the quality of any discussion. Your role is rather to facilitate the group to evaluate its own ideas.
- A summary presents an overview of discussion acknowledging the range of views or ideas while highlighting the main issues. Check with the group or the individual that your summary is accurate and acceptable to them before moving on.

Materials required:
- Flip chart.
- Overhead projector.
- Coloured pens.

Technique:	<div align="center">**Giving feedback**</div>

Purpose:
- To enhance learning by an individual or group.
- To help them evaluate a course of action or decision.
- To enhance self-awareness.

Tips for use:
- Give formal feedback only as part of a procedure or programme agreed with the group.
- Most people respond to praise, encouragement and recognition.
- If you preface negative feedback with a positive statement, it is usually received more favourably.
- Feedback should be directed only at things the group or individual can do something about.
- Detailed feedback gives more opportunity for learning than broad, general statements.
- Allow the other person to accept or reject your feedback – you cannot impose your beliefs or opinions on others.
- Offer suggestions for improving on more negative areas.
- Ask for the group's or individual's ideas on how they might effect some change.
- Take responsibility for feedback that you give, say 'I think' or 'In my opinion'.

A useful format to follow when giving feedback might be:

1 Facilitator and group or individual recap on what took place.
2 Clarify any matters of fact.
3 The group or individual describes what went well.
4 The Facilitator discusses what was achieved.
5 The group or individual discusses which tasks were not achieved and makes recommendations as to how they might have been achieved.
6 The Facilitator discusses which tasks were not achieved and makes recommendations as to how they might have been achieved.
7 Any differences of opinion are discussed and, if possible, resolved.
8 The group or individual is left with a clear knowledge of strengths and of specific changes which might lead to improvement.

Chapter 6

The Facilitator as change agent

Summary

In this chapter we will bring together many of the ideas already discussed, and summarise the key messages of the book.

Sections of this chapter highlight:

- the challenge of change in primary care
- facilitation as a change management skill
- the profile of a Facilitator
- understanding organisations
- factors affecting the acceptance and implementation of change
- managing a process of structured organisational development
- a process for reflection.

You may find it useful to read this chapter first. Alternatively, if you have read through the book chronologically, this chapter should help to establish the main points in your mind or stimulate you to revisit certain sections.

Please bear in mind that becoming more facilitative or acting effectively in the formal Facilitator role requires skills which need time and practice to develop. Personal qualities and individual style play a significant part. No two Facilitators operate in exactly the same way.

Building on the principles of facilitating groups in primary care, the subject of volume 1 in this series (Duffy and Griffin, 1999), our aim in this *manual has been to heighten your awareness of the individual and organisational factors which play a significant part in the change process, so that as a Facilitator you can effectively diagnose a situation, or characterise an organisation and so properly target any help or intervention. We have incorporated a range of tools which have been proved useful in various settings.*

The challenge of managing change in primary care

Change, relentless in pace and demanding in nature, is ever present in the modern-day National Health Service. In recent times the introduction of clinical governance, patient participation, primary care groups and local healthcare co-operatives have required new structures and processes to be designed, new ways of working to be effected. Many of those charged with the design and implementation of these initiatives and new organisations have predominantly clinical backgrounds and little, if any, formal education in organisational development. Some individuals may be facilitative by nature but many will bring vested interests, or try to wield power associated with their professional status. Others will be jaded with the demands of constant change and most will be focused on the task in hand – on satisfying performance criteria, complying with legislation or fulfilling political requirements.

Facilitation as a change-management skill

Our belief is that facilitation, as a useful life skill for all working in primary care, has the potential to guide, structure and smooth the processes involved in these new ways of working, and that Facilitators, or facilitative individuals, can stimulate, motivate and support the individuals and groups concerned.

Many new facilitation posts have been created: audit facilitators, clinical governance facilitators, practice development facilitators, primary care group facilitators; but, equally, posts otherwise labelled, e.g. local healthcare co-operative manager, or clinical effectiveness co-ordinator, are demanding demonstrable facilitation skills in their incumbents.

What will these Facilitators need? It is equally important to ask how any of us involved in the NHS, with a part to play in developing practice, improving quality, designing guidelines or encouraging new collaborative working relationships, can act in a more facilitative way to manage the changes required.

The modern conception of a 'change agent' gives more emphasis to possession of interpersonal and managerial skills in communication, influencing and negotiation than to the traditional content skills or specialist technical expertise. Hutton's description of an effective change agent sounds much like our descriptions of the perfect primary care Facilitator:

> *Does not have to walk on water but . . . should be patient, persistent, honest, trustworthy, reliable, positive, enthusiastic, co-operative, confident (but not arrogant), a good listener, observant (of the feelings and behaviours of others), flexible, resourceful, difficult to intimidate, willing to take risks and accept challenge and be able to handle organisational politics. And they should have a sense of humour, a sense of perspective and be able to admit ignorance and ask for help when appropriate.*
>
> Hutton (1994)

The profile of a Facilitator

At a recent training course for key players in the delivery of the clinical governance agenda in Scotland (Royal College of General Practitioners (Scotland), Practical Clinical Effectiveness Course, Dunkeld, 1999), a 'light went on' in the mind of one doctor after participating in a training session on Facilitation skills: 'Now I can see it. You really have to be something of a performer. You need to generate energy, radiate enthusiasm, motivate people and sustain a positive, upbeat tone.' Dr Muir Gray, a keynote speaker at a recent conference entitled 'Facilitation and the new NHS' (National Primary Care Facilitation Programme Conference, Facilitation in Primary Care, London, 1998), described the Facilitator as requiring 'charismatic relentlessness'. Others have coined the phrase 'the peaceful warrior'.

In many ways it may be easier to act out this role when you are external to the organisation or the group, and when your title reflects the Facilitator role; but whether internal or external, we suggest that you need the same well-defined personal qualities and traits (for more details, see Duffy and Griffin, 1999):

- flexibility of style
- respect for the autonomy of others
- honesty, reliability
- neutrality and objectivity
- sensitivity to others, empathy
- caring, warmth and genuineness in approach
- enthusiasm and positive attitude to the job in hand

and that you will require knowledge of the context and of group processes, and well-developed skills in:

- providing orientation and structure in the course of work
- identifying useful resources
- using techniques and tools for interpersonal and group management and development
- dealing with conflict.

You will make use of a range of basic facilitation techniques, including:

- ice-breaking
- brainstorming
- setting objectives
- summarising
- clarifying the task and process of groups
- agreeing appropriate decision-making techniques
- creative problem solving.

You will be able to intervene in a facilitative and respectful way and you will have the knowledge and experience to select, modify where necessary, and use effectively, a range of tools to help your particular group manage change successfully.

Understanding organisations

Building on the foundations of volume 1 (Duffy and Griffin, 1999), which focused on groups and how to facilitate them effectively, we have concentrated in this volume on developing your understanding of people in organisations and your appreciation of how both individual and organisational factors can either aid or inhibit successful change management and outcomes.

We have identified how the structure of an organisation, with its seats of power and lines of accountability, can affect the motivation and performance of individuals. In a very fundamental way, we resonate with the theory that individuals have basic needs which have to be met within their organisations in order to allow them to function at a higher intellectual and more effective interpersonal level. We have observed how poor management of change has the potential to damage an individual's experience of psychological success, and that those who perceive others to hold control over their lives may feel powerless in the change process. Both individual and organisational life cycles can have an impact on the management of change. Equally challenging is that organisations and individuals are continuously dynamic. As Facilitators, establishing and maintaining cognisance of key organisational features will help us design, manage and review change processes appropriate to the specific setting.

General practice, while obviously different in essence from more business-oriented cultures, nevertheless exhibits a multitude of forms, where every practice or grouping displays a unique combination of structure, culture and people, all subtly changing over time, shaped by both external and internal forces. Whether we think of an organisation as a machine, an organism, a brain, or even a psychic prison, any Facilitator will need to find ways of making sense of that organisation's structure, culture and members' behaviours in order to work effectively with the organisation in the medium or longer term. That defining or diagnosing process should supplement a general understanding of the various aspects of change management which require attention or clarification.

Accepting and implementing change

Research shows that individuals will accept change if:

- they can see some advantage to themselves in doing so
- the change is compatible with what currently happens
- it is not too complex
- it can be adopted gradually
- they can see that it works.

Problems in *implementing* change can arise from organisational factors:

- unclear aims of the organisation
- ineffective leadership
- unassertive management
- negative climate
- inappropriate structure
- unbalanced power relationships
- undeveloped individuals
- ineffective teamwork

or where the change-management strategy fits poorly with the prevailing culture, particularly in relation to how individual members are typically motivated to change.

Individuals can resist change due to:

- denial
- blind spots
- avoidance
- projection
- lack of readiness
- no shared model for change management
- change perceived as arbitrary
- overemphasis of rationality.

A facilitative approach to change management

A more facilitative approach to groupworking helps in the change-management process, as does structured planning, implementation and review of change processes, through:

- encouraging planning for change
- exploring worries about the impact of change
- diagnosing barriers to change
- dealing with conflict in a group
- encouraging collaboration in managing a change
- effecting progress with implementation of change
- identifying and agreeing responsibilities for implementing change.

We have suggested tools and techniques designed to help at each of these stages.

Managing a programme of structured organisational development

When managing a *programme of structured organisational development*, rather than focusing on one changing aspect of an organisation's function, the need for an accurate characterisation or a diagnosis of that organisation becomes critical. We have suggested a number of techniques and tools to diagnose the effectiveness of the teamwork, to identify the training needs of individual members, to rate the performance of the practice organisation across the broad areas of caring, communication, planning and management, and to reach a consensus on the strengths and weaknesses of the practice. We also describe a new process developed in Dundee (Duffy *et al.*, 1998), where information gathered via a range of diagnostic processes aids the characterisation of a practice such that development-linked interventions can be timed and targeted effectively. This **Practice Characterisation Model** assesses a practice's

- stability
- current coping ability
- culture of change management
- readiness to face the challenge of change

and suggests that practices with different profiles may well benefit from a variety of interim development activities or support before engaging in a full-blown, team-based practice development programme.

In such a planned, large-scale programme, the Facilitator can help the practice visualise the ideal, create the future and plan to achieve it. She can also support the change processes and encourage review of progress and impact. A key component of these and other facilitative activities will be her personal own reflection and review, informed by others' feedback on her performance.

We leave you with a suggested format for reviewing your own performance (see below) and end this volume with the story of the Gold Practice – a real-life suburban practice, required to produce for the first time a detailed practice development plan but lacking both insight into its own organisation and the skills necessary to obtain and use such information in a systematic way in order to write the plan.

We hope you have found this volume useful and wish you well, Facilitators and ordinary team members alike, in the challenging task of working effectively with others in order to manage change successfully.

A process for reflection

1 **Description:** *What happened?*
   - Recall the experience as soon after the event as possible, and write down a description of what happened.

2 **Feelings:** *What were you thinking and feeling?*
   - How aware of the experience were you?
   - What were you thinking?
   - What assumptions did you make and how valid were they?
   - What were you feeling?
   - What were your own attitudes and feelings in this situation?
   - What aspects of your own behaviour were you aware of?

3. **Evaluation:** *What was good and bad about the experience?*
   - What is your interpretation of this situation at present? (Such as 'a waste of time', 'being used', 'not being up to the mark', 'a job well done'.)
   - Include justifications for your interpretations, for example what factors and knowledge are influencing your judgement?
   - Did you recognise these as forming a pattern or echoing previous experience?

4 **Analysis:** *What sense can you make of the situation?*
   - We sometimes criticise others to take attention away from our own perceived inadequacies; therefore watch any tendency to make judgements, either about others or yourself. Re-evaluate the experience by comparing what you know and feel already about this situation, with other possible related causes. For instance, rather than concentrating on the negative or obstructive feelings and events, focus on the positive aspect of the situation.

5 **Conclusion:** *What else could you have done?*
   - How do I now feel about this experience?
   - How could I have dealt better with this situation?
   - What would have been the consequences of these other choices?

6 **Action plan:** *If it arose again, what would you do?*
   - What have I learned from the experience?
   - How would I ensure that my practice was going to change for the better, in a similar situation?

Case Study 9
The Gold Practice: facilitating education and development

Key players:

Dr A, male	Nearing retirement, kindly but winding down, still deferred to because of position, unused to modern teamworking, displays traditional qualities of paternalism, conservatism.
Dr B, male	Quiet, late 40s, focused on patients, scared of modern technology, prefers to avoid conflict, polite but distant.
Dr C, female	Returner after a long career break, struggling to settle in and get fully up to speed.
Mrs D, practice manager	Previously senior receptionist, keen to take on more of a managerial role, has begun a Diploma in Management but tends to be bogged down with nitty gritty administrative tasks. No real job description but given respect, if not much power, by the partners.
Mrs E, practice nurse	Not invited to management meetings, keen and enthusiastic practitioner, has broadened skills to encompass counselling and asthma management. Would like to formalise chronic disease management within the practice.
Mrs F, health visitor	Involved in a variety of local nursing and research groups, e.g. bereavement counselling and sleep study, but finds practice computer statistics difficult to access and not compatible with those of other practices. Tends to do her own thing. Not involved in management meetings.
Mrs G, district nurse	Very busy with the older patients, who form a high percentage of the practice population. Enjoys company of other nursing staff in the practice, but this is largely at a social level. Not involved in management meetings.
Practice receptionists	Work well as a team, but feel they have little influence on the current or future development of the practice.

On the basis of structured observation, interviews with all members of the practice team and discussion based around a feedback report, the Facilitator worked with the practice at an 'away-day' and helped them reach agreement on their current strengths and weaknesses.

Here is a selection from their agreed strengths:

- Happy, relaxed atmosphere
- All enjoy working in the practice
- The practice has experienced and coped with a major organisational upheaval
- People respect each other and have a reasonable understanding of each other's roles
- The administrative side is well organised along a task basis
- The practice manager's role has developed and she is respected by all in the practice
- The GPs have confidence in the ability of the practice nurses; the practice nurses are generally seen as professionals in their own right
- The skills and interests of the three partners are quite complementary
- There are practice meetings although on an occasional basis
- Availability of patient appointments is excellent
- Face-to-face communication is effective

Some of the potential weaknesses were agreed to be:

- There is a big shortage of space and people are overcrowded
- GPs were reluctant to share their views on the implications for the practice with the rest of the team
- There could be greater understanding by the practice of the actual duties and activities of the district nursing and health visiting staff
- The practice manager's role has just evolved; the doctors have not defined their expectations of her and the practice manager has skills which are not being utilised
- The role of the practice nurse could be extended, but this requires motivation by the nurses and direction from the GPs
- The partners are at different stages in their respective lives and this will soon impact on the practice's future; to date it has not been discussed
- Meetings have tended to be rambling, decisions unclear and agreed actions often not carried through
- Patient numbers are dropping. This has not been addressed formally
- The computer software is peculiar to the practice. The partner who designed it will be retiring soon

The goals for the next 2–3 years were set that day. These were:

- to identify suitable new premises for the practice
- to invest in, and use effectively, a new computer network

- to develop systematically the organisation of the practice such that skills and knowledge are used most efficiently
- to improve formal communication systems within the practice
- to extend the range of services offered to patients
- to structure and implement a chronic disease management programme.

The Facilitator then helped the practice with a number of 'process activities' which would later prove to be key in their efforts towards achieving their goals. She:

- facilitated a discussion between the partners and practice manager on the role of the practice manager
- gave written and practical guidance on improving practice meetings, leading by example at the first two meetings following the practice development 'away-day'
- identified three useful local training days for practice members: Meeting Skills, Information Management and Technology, and Sharing Clinical Work Effectively
- supported the practice manager in writing the practice development plan, which was to be their working document
- encouraged the practice to review progress every 3 months or so and congratulate themselves on any achievements
- made herself available to the practice, at their request, for any advice, support or guidance they felt to be necessary.

In short, she provided *'the opportunity, resources, encouragement and support for the group to succeed in achieving its own objectives and to do this through enabling the group to take control and responsibility for the way it proceeded'* (Bentley 1994). This would seem to us to be a good working definition of facilitation – a process which, in this practice, helped it to both construct a development plan and make considerable progress toward achieving the priorities contained within it.

References

Argyris C (1964) *Integrating the Individual and the Organisation.* Wiley, Chichester.

Bartram S and Gibson B (1994) *Training Needs Analysis.* Gower Publishing, Aldershot.

Bentley T (1994) *Facilitation. Providing Opportunities for Learning.* McGraw Hill, London.

Buchanan D and Huczynski A (1997) *Organisational Behaviour: An Introductory Text.* Prentice Hall, London.

Chell E (1993) *The Psychology of Behaviour in Organisations.* Macmillan, London.

Crombie IK, Davies HTO, Abraham SCS and Florey C duV (1993) *The Audit Handbook: Improving Health Care Through Clinical Audit.* John Wiley & Sons, Chichester.

Duffy M and Griffin E (1998) *Facilitation Skills Training Workshop.* Tayside Centre for General Practice, University of Dundee.

Duffy M and Griffin E (1999) *Facilitating Groups in Primary Care.* Radcliffe Medical Press, Oxford.

Duffy M, Griffin E and Bain J (1998) *Facilitating Education and Development for Practice Development Planning: The FED Project – Final Report.* Tayside Centre for General Practice, University of Dundee, Dundee.

Erikson E (1977) *Childhood and Society.* Triad/Granada, London.

Grant J, Napier A, Stephen S *et al.* (1998) Integrating audit into primary care: a Tayside initiative. *Health Bulletin* **56**(5): 822–7.

Griffin E, Sanders C, Craven D and King J (2000) Development and evaluation of a computerised 360° feedback tool for general practice. *Health Informatics Journal.* **6**(2): 71–80.

Handy C (1993) *Understanding Organisations* (4e). Penguin Books, London.

Hart L (1992) *The Faultless Facilitator.* Kogan Page, London.

Hunter D, Bailey A and Taylor B (1996) *The Facilitation of Groups.* Gower, Aldershot.

Hutton D (1994) *The Change Agent's Handbook: A Survival Guide for Quality Improvement Champions.* ASQC Quality Press, Milwaukee, Wisconsin.

Maslow A (1954) *Motivation and Personality.* Harper-Row, New York.

Mathew D (1994) *Change Technique.* King's Fund College, London.

Morgan G (1997) *Images of Organization.* Sage, London.

Nilson C (1993) *Team Games for Trainers.* McGraw-Hill, London.

Phares J (1976) *Locus of Control in Personality.* General Learning Press, Morristown, New Jersey.

Plovnick M, Fry R and Rubin I (1978) *Managing Health Care Delivery. A training programme for primary care physicians.* Ballinger Publishing, Cambridge, Massachusetts.

Pollitt C (1996) Business approaches to quality improvement: why they are hard for the NHS to swallow. *Quality in Health Care* **5**: 104–10.

Pritchard P and Pritchard J (1994) *Teamwork for Primary and Shared Care – A Practical Workbook* (2e). Oxford Medical Publications, Oxford.

Rasberry RW and Lindsay LL (1994) *Effective Managerial Communication* (2e). Wadsworth Publications, Belmont, California.

Rotter JR (1966) Generalised expectations for internal versus external control of reinforcement. *Psychological Monographs* **80**(1).

Savage Young and Associates *The Community Nurse Development Programme.* Edinburgh.

Scott M and Marinker M (1993) Managing change in general practice. In M Pringle (ed) *Change and Teamwork in Primary Care*. BMJ Publications, London.

Spiegal N, Murphy E, Kinmonth AL *et al.* (1992) Managing change in general practice: a step by step guide. *BMJ* **304**: 231–4.

Strauss A and Corbin J (1990) *Basics of Qualitative Research*. SAGE Publications, Newbury Park, California.

The Scottish Office, Department of Health (1997) *Designed to Care: Renewing the National Health Service in Scotland*. The Stationery Office, Edinburgh.

The Welsh Office (1997) *The 'IT' Files – General Practice Computing Demonstration Project*. The Stationery Office, Cardiff.

Wilson A (1994) *Changing Practices in Primary Care: A Facilitator's Handbook*. Health Education Authority, London.

Woodcock M and Francis D (1981) *Organisational Development through Teambuilding*. Gower, Aldershot.